LONDON

The Dog Who Made the Team

By DAVID MALCOLMSON

DUELL, SLOAN AND PEARCE

New York

First edition

Duell, Sloan & Pearce

Affiliate of
MEREDITH PRESS
Des Moines & New York

MANUFACTURED IN THE UNITED STATES OF AMERICA FOR MEREDITH PRESS

VAN REES PRESS • NEW YORK

To E.

Contents

CHAPTER		PAGE
1.	Dog and Man	3
2.	London Lends a Hand	11
3.	A Bat in the Face	19
4.	London Gets His Contract	27
5.	London Meets the Team	37
6.	Play Ball	44
7.	Rhubarb	55
8.	Home Run	66
9.	Camera!	74
10.	Dog Star	90

LONDON

The Dog Who Made the Team

CHAPTER ONE

Dog and Man

IT TOOK a baseball bat," sometimes Chuck will say, "to knock this kind of sense into London's head." But he only pretends that London's talent came through an outside force.

Of course it did not. The dread accident of the bat, while the two were playing ball together in the park—which Chuck has never been able to forget—served chiefly to open the man's eyes. London's genius was already there, hidden within him, just as it lies unrealized in any good dog. What has made London unique among great dogs is the result of a man's awakening.

The circumstances were right. For a time a man and a dog lived only for each other. It began when everything Chuck had worked for in this world was suddenly taken from him. The Chicago White Sox let him go. All the ability and determination that had made him a big-league pitcher were thereupon focused on his dog. It happened too at a time when the dog was at just the right age to begin his great love, ten months old. After the unhappy accident, which nearly cost London his life, the two became inseparable.

Chuck swore he would never leave him again so long as he lived. He lost his own sense of failure in making it up to London for the blow he had dealt him. London responded in a way far beyond anything Chuck could have expected. As a result Chuck Eisenmann, with London, found a new career crowned by success beyond his highest hopes in the world of baseball.

As a boy on a dairy farm he had dreamed of a great pitching arm. Milking cows was but a way of building strength into his right hand and into his right forearm. He threw stones. He threw balls. Always he aimed at a target. As he threw a rock, a clod, an apple even, he planned for each finger to do its part, to give a ball a needed twist. A baseball must speed from finger tips straight as an arrow for the first sixty feet of its flight, then curve down and out at last to frustrate the batter waiting to swat it. Putting mind and soul and body into his right arm, he built an arm he could take to any manager in the land and say, "Step out on the diamond and see for yourself."

A war injury was the probable source of his downfall. A bomb blast in London left him with a hurt elbow. He learned to work that arm again, able to pitch nine full innings, until the day of his crack-up with the Chicago White Sox.

That was a day!

On that midseason afternoon, the Sox were headed for the cellar again. Chuck, who was one of the twelve pitchers thus far to survive every cut, was sitting on a bench, away down in the bull pen, watching Detroit clobber his teammates. In Comisky Park that bench is so far from the pitcher's mound, where Chuck was so eager to be, that Chicago maintained a jeep just to bring in relief pitchers. Away down the left-field foul line he sat.

He no longer cared how much they paid him. A good pitcher needs to perform. He has to make himself part of the record. Once he had averaged twelve strike-outs a game. Like any actor a ball-player needs to keep showing his audience what he can do.

"How come I don't pitch?" But he already knew the answer; his field manager was himself in trouble with the general manager up front; he liked Chuck's pitching; but the general manager was playing favorites.

The field manager said, "You got to show something."

"I show more in batting practice than the men you are using show in this game."

"Oh, yeah? So what? Anybody does better in practice than when he's up against the real thing."

Chuck had too quick an answer; he should have stopped to think. Sarcastically he taunted, "It would be nice if you had something to say about running this ball club."

Once again the White Sox were aimed at second division, way down in the bottom half. Heads were about to fall. "I run this team, Eisenmann." The field manager was red in the face. "And I run it my way." He turned on a heel.

Even then Chuck did not let him off the hook. "You run us all right!" he shouted. "Right into the cellar again." He should never have said that. "And all because you won't use your best talent."

The manager swung around. "Meaning you!" Hands on hips he looked his scorn.

It was a bad day from beginning to end. During the seventh inning, in a game now hopelessly lost, the score twelve to two with Detroit on the long end, the manager telephoned the bull pen.

"Eisenmann, you're it. You're so good. Then get 'em out in the eighth and ninth." And he banged the receiver.

"Okay!" yelled Chuck regardless.

At the moment Detroit was in the field. The White Sox had one man out, two on.

Any pitcher has to be given time to warm up with a lot of practice throws, even with the most dependable pitching arm. That's the function of a bull pen—a place for pitchers to warm up. Normally before he is called in from the pen he takes a minimum of twenty-five warmup pitches. A few slow, a few fast, a few curves, a few fork balls, any other pet throws, until he is ready to go on.

Hardly had Chuck grabbed up his glove when a double play retired the Sox.

The game could not wait. Before eight thousand listless fans who had already made their opinion of the game overly clear, the umpire motioned him in.

Chuck walked briskly to the mound, furtively rubbing his elbow in an attempt to loosen tendons. It had never been his habit to talk about his injury. His elbow was his problem, he would solve it himself, lest he become known as a pitcher with a bum arm. He did not patronize the team doctor but hired his own specialist.

It was not as though he would have to pitch completely cold. After he is on the mound a pitcher gets eight more warmup pitches. If it is an emergency he takes as many as he needs. But since Chuck was simply a reliefer, called in at the whim of a manager, near the end of a game already lost, this hardly qualified as an emergency. Eight times he gingerly threw the ball, trying to loosen a cold elbow.

"Play ball!"

In his meager warmup he had not dared try the breaking curve which was his trade-mark.

A batter was up. Chuck could not even find the plate. Four balls. The man walked.

The next batter pulled Chuck's change-of-pace to third. It should have made an easy catch. The third baseman booted it.

Nobody out. Two were on.

Against the third batter Chuck worked the count to two strikes, three balls. Now he had to get the ball over with something on it. He had to throw his great curve. Thousands were watching, and not in sympathy, as he pulled at the back of his cap, blew damp air from his mouth onto his pitching fingers. He took a glance at the runner at first, stepped off the rubber and began pawing the dirt with his cleats. He stepped back on the rubber, pulled his cap lower, peered for the catcher's sign, nodded, and wound up.

Everything he had went into his overhand drop. The ball left his finger tips destined to behave precisely as intended.

"Strike three!"

The man was out.

But back on the mound a fiery pain was flashing bad news. Chuck felt he was going to be sick.

Had this been a routine occasion he would have made his damage known. Nobody would expect him to pitch even one more ball under the circumstances. Today was different. Today nothing could force him to beg for mercy.

The rest of the eighth was a nightmare. One was out. Chuck forced his arm to throw the ball. His elbow no longer made sense. A man walked. Another. One came in.

By now the manager must have recognized Chuck's trouble, no matter how piqued he was. Yet when Chuck looked back to the bull pen it was to look in vain. Nobody was warming up. He walked three men in a row. They cost twelve torturous throws. Still no relief was in sight.

It was up to him to plan his own strategy of desperation. He would get batters out by throwing his change-of-pace, nothing fancy, aimed only at putting the ball legally over the plate, tempting the Tigers to hit him. Hit him they did. Any kid could have swatted those cunnythumb throws.

It worked, but not until seven runs were scored in the eighth of that gruesome game. At long last, through the co-operation of the outfield, men making long circus catches, they got the side out. The score was now 19–2 for Detroit.

At the dugout the manager was waiting for him. "And you're the guy with the so great talent."

He refused to plead his case. Next day, called on the carpet, he did not roll up his sleeve, to bare a swelling that would make any trainer in the land place him on the injured list. Nor would he apologize to the field manager.

The White Sox did not let him go; he was good property; he would be farmed out. Rather than fizzle out down the line, Chuck requested his release.

He was given his pink slip. He was out, as cut off from his past as on that day when, after the war, he had been honorably discharged from the Army. Of his arm his doctor could only say, "We'll have to wait and see. Take it easy, Chuck. Why don't you open a restaurant?"

In all the world he could think of no single person he cared to face. He might have flown north to his mother. She lived in a Wisconsin town, now that Pa had died and the farm was gone. Ma would give him boundless sympathy.

"Poor Cholly."

He could see her rock back and forth, regarding him.

"Cholly, better you settle down. With Emil a nice job in the garage. Here at home with Emil. Here with George."

The last thing Chuck wanted was to become "Poor Cholly."

Westward in California two upstairs rooms were being held against his return. The family he rented them from while he played winter ball in the Southland was also keeping for him a German shepherd pup he had bought eight months before. Helen, daughter of the house, had been sending him snapshots showing the dog's growth. Chuck had to talk out his problem to somebody, even if it was only to a nine-month-old dog. Because of London, Los Angeles became his haven.

From the Los Angeles airport he did not go immediately to his rooms. No one was expecting him, with the ball season still on. An airport limousine took him first to Pasadena where he had stored

his convertible. He came within an inch of selling the car, of blowing in his money on a new automobile. Better give his spirit a boost than lie back and watch his money slowly melt away.

But his faith in his comeback was not strong enough for the new car. It was the old yellow convertible, though waxed and serviced, with chrome gleaming, that he drove to his rooms and parked under the eucalyptus tree.

There was a new plastic awning over his upstairs window. It made him surer of himself. Even so, he stood a while in silence at the front door before he pushed the button.

Somewhere within he thought he heard a bark. He rang.

The door opened, and the dog was right there upon him. A gangling half-grown monster crowded in front of Helen. It did not seem possible the pup could have grown so much in so short a time. Here was a stiff-eared German shepherd no stranger would be wise to disregard.

"Hi, Helen."

"Chuck! It's you!"

Had this high-school girl been his little sister he would have put his arm around her and picked her up and kissed her, just to let her know how glad he was to be welcomed. Instead he stood staring at the dog.

When that defender saw, from Helen's attitude, how the man was no mere bell-ringing solicitor, he demanded his share of the excitement, raising both paws to Chuck's light gabardines.

If there is one unmannerly trick to mark the ill-trained dog, it is this habit of putting paws, clean or dirty, on a visitor's clothing.

"Get down!" Chuck shoved him hard. In surprise London retreated behind the girl, uncertain what to make of it.

Helen turned back to London. "It's all right, honey. He's just not glad to see us. It's all right with us, though, isn't it?"

London agreed. So it was up to Chuck to apologize.

"Helen, you know I'm glad to see you. And I sure do appreciate what you've done for us. Just look at him, Helen. Boy, what a great dog he's going to be!"

Down on his knees, Chuck took hold of both sides of London's face. He told himself he must not get soft now, he would not give Helen a long story of why he was here, in midseason. He wasn't going to expose himself to this girl's sympathy, any more than he would to his mother's.

"We do appreciate her, don't we, London. Boy, how you've grown!"

With his cheeks held firmly in Chuck's big hands, London could not hide his embarrassment. Chuck looked up at Helen. "You've grown too, you know. Big girl now."

Then it began. It started with London's nose. The strong grip of the man, close under his ears, must have carried an odor the dog had never quite forgotten. It took but time for that dear scent to awaken a fuller memory. Suddenly his whole body wagged. The heavy plumed tail waved wildly. London knew who their caller was. When Chuck let him go, he leaped upon him.

"Get down! Don't put your feet up!" But Chuck was laughing loudly. "It's going to take a good man to handle you!"

"I'm ready!" declared London's dancing eyes. "I remember you."

CHAPTER TWO

London Lends a Hand

THAT FIRST NIGHT London slept with Chuck on a bed narrow for two large bodies. Neither slept well. London did his best to lie still, but his legs jerked. Three times, as Chuck rolled over, London was tumbled to the floor. Finally the dog left the uneasy bed to wander into the living room and curl up on the sofa.

At three o'clock he was back at Chuck's side.

"Hmm, hmm, hmm," he insisted in his smallest voice.

Chuck opened his eyes and considered him.

London struck the side of the bed with a heavy paw. "Get up. You've got to take me. You always did."

Downstairs they went, barefoot into the night.

When morning came, Chuck told London, "I know a man to see about my arm. He's a bone specialist in Beverly Hills. Used to be on the staff of the Giants." He not only wanted to talk; he half-believed that, if he talked to his dog as a person, in time London would come to understand. It's the way a child learns the language. All sorts of things are said to a baby; and all at once he knows what is being told him. "While we're getting this arm back into shape, you and I are going to play a lot of ball together. By the time winter ball begins I'll be able to pitch every Sunday. Want to go for a ride?"

These last words, at least, London understood. He put an eager paw on Chuck's knee. Of course he wanted to, if Chuck was going.

Chuck held open the car door. London leaped onto the back seat. When Chuck slid under the wheel he changed to the front seat, to sit up as tall as the man at his side.

In Beverly Hills Chuck parked in the shade of the medical building and turned to his companion.

"His office is in this building. I won't be long. Now look here, fellow. It's going to be warm with the top up. Listen to me. I'm leaving you parked in the shade. Even so these windows ought to be left open. Do you suppose you can stay in this car alone and behave yourself?"

London answered with so intelligent a look that he must have understood.

Just to be doubly sure, Chuck added the command, "Stay!"

But when he stepped to the street and started to close the door behind him, London made it clear he did not understand he was to be left alone. He held his nose down to keep the door open. He was not going to risk losing his man all over again.

Chuck shoved his head back and slammed the door. "I said, 'Stay!' "

When he reached the sidewalk, London was in his own place but with head and shoulders thrust out the partly closed window.

"Don't you try that." Chuck walked deliberately on, refusing to look back at him.

The dog in the car, deserted on a street where strangers were hurrying back and forth and automobiles sped by, was utterly alone. He noted how the driver's window was wide open. He placed forepaws on the ledge. Hind legs gave the needed thrust. A flying leap landed him on the street, in the path of traffic, and he raced to the sidewalk. With joy he saw his man reappear, hurrying to meet him.

Chuck grabbed him by the scruff; with one hand he lifted his fifty pounds clear of the walk. To a dog this feat is an impressive form of punishment. In a wolf pack only a super-leader would be strong enough to discipline an adolescent with this masterful method. It is the way a dog mother picks up a helpless pup. Holding London by the fold of loose skin, Chuck shook him. It impressed London. Chuck meant it to impress him.

"Ow! ow-ow-ow!"

People on the sidewalk were outraged. "Young man," declared an elderly purple-haired woman, "I hope he bites you!" But city people do not really interfere. They look instead for the police, who are never there when needed.

Chuck dragged his dog back to the car, opened the door, and hurled him in.

"When I tell you, 'Stay!' I mean stay!"

Even so, Chuck would not roll up those windows. To do so would be his confession of failure. It was up to London to learn what was expected of him.

"Stay!"

Just let him jump out that window again!

London still could not believe he meant it. He studied the retreating figure through half-closed eyes. When Chuck reached the entrance and rounded the corner to pass from sight, he leaped. Once again he landed on the street. Automobile brakes squealed. Tail between his legs he made for the sidewalk. And there was Chuck, running toward him.

This time the man's manner showed the dog his mistake. He turned back to the yellow convertible. From the sidewalk he leaped, clearing a window hardly wide enough to admit his body, a beautiful, impossible vault into their car. He sat in his place, eyes front, and waited.

Somebody laughed.

A man nodded approval at Chuck. After all, even the most sentimental dog-lover can see that punishment must not be left to speeding vehicles. In a man's city a dog can be killed for his failure to obey.

Chuck stood by the car, looking in. London was trying to tell him, by the way he sat so proudly upright, that he would never again jump out. Leave the door open, Chuck. Try me. Walk away. This time I'll show you. Okay?

Chuck looked at him, undecided. Then, for a third time, he went to the medical building. Out he popped again, to see London still in his place, looking straight ahead.

Chuck would not risk it. He went back to roll the windows high, leaving space only for air.

The discouraging days of Chuck's dragged-out therapy found London's higher education in full swing. Already his physical age was that of a six-year-old boy; his mental age was higher. Since baseball had been the teacher's life, their major subject was baseball. Even before Chuck had entered the Chisox spring-training camp, leaving a four-month-old London with Helen, he had tried to share with his little dog something of his love for the game. The infant could barely manage a tennis ball then. Chuck had rolled a regulation baseball to him and laughed as he tried to close his mouth over the round hardness. In their kindergarten play the little fellow had taken Chuck's baseball between his paws, to gnaw with needle teeth at leather saturated with the smell of Chuck's hand, raising a light eyebrow as he regarded his big mentor. Even at that early age adult hair had begun to show through the brown baby fur of his coat, his tail bushing out. At four months his coat was dark with a hint of rust, offset by those white bands back of his shoulder blades. At that age he had also learned the rudiments of discipline.

Chuck had been reading . . .

When he looked down from the *Sporting News,* the little fellow was still on his white rug, but now, down there on the floor, instead of gnawing at Chuck's ball, he had Chuck's pitcher's glove.

"Hey!"

Too late. Already a hole had been chewed wetly between forefinger and the long middle finger. This five-fingered glove was the one possession Chuck never let any teammate touch. It had been his favorite glove since before the war. He owned a new glove too, but it did not have the right feel.

"Look what you've done!" Anger sharpened his voice. He took hold of the pup's snout and pushed the chewed glove into his face.

"Yipe—eip—eip—eip!"

Though Chuck kept this old glove soft with neat's-foot oil, the leather was cracked. The back needed resewing. He had restrung the finger webbing. The pocket had been pounded thin as a pancake by numberless caught balls. "Put it on the griddle and fry it," the boys said about Chuck's old glove. Now a hole was chewed between the fingers.

"You've got your own things to play with. Next time you'll get a shaking!"

The puppy jumped up to lick Chuck's face and be forgiven. If only he could put his whimpers into words. "Don't be mad at me. Say you like me. But now! Do you still like me? Pick me up, okay?"

Chuck picked him up. After all, he could mend the old glove once more. London covered his face with kisses, his heart beating wildly. He licked Chuck's neck and tried to bury his face under his arm.

"You'll have to learn not to touch things that don't belong to you."

Now that London was almost a year old he learned fast.

At playing catch his timing was better than a man's. A hard-pitched tennis ball he could take smack in his mouth and rush it back to Chuck's hand. With a baseball Chuck had to be careful of his teeth. He was able to slice a baseball with his bat to make it slow on the bounce. From the way it hit the ground London figured the angle. Up he reared, to take the ball well back in his mouth where teeth were strong and firmly anchored.

Some things the pupil did better than the teacher. At the playground, when a batted ball rolled under the backstop and lost itself in the weeds, Chuck would have had to spend more time searching, parting the long grass, than the ball was worth. London simply circled the area on a trot. He turned when his nose told him to turn; in less than a minute his keen nose touched the ball before his eyes saw it.

For this he was praised to the skies.

At home, in their rooms, London often tried to get Chuck to talk to him. He seemed to know when his man was depressed about his arm.

Chuck was sitting without even a magazine, just rubbing his elbow. London dropped their baseball into his lap.

"You know, Lon," soon Chuck began, "the leather that covers a baseball is cut to form two matched figure eights. No other flat design can be stitched so well around a sphere." London was fascinated, and anyone who thinks that nothing of the man's feeling came through to him is wrong. "When I pitch, Lon, my upper finger has to reach for this seam. The seam gives me control. With finger and thumb on the seams I can throw a ball a hundred miles an hour, from mound to home plate, and control its curve within inches as it drops away from a bat."

London did not find him boastful. He took their baseball into his wide jaws, tossed it back into Chuck's lap, and stood there, worshipping the man who would take the trouble to talk to him.

"Okay, boy, we'll go for a walk, then."

From the way Chuck took off his robe, he knew they really would go for a walk. London knew every article of Chuck's clothing. How he loved to see shoelaces being tied!

A dog's brain is a big brain. Like a man's, only part of it is ever called into use. Sometimes it is said dogs read people's minds. It is more than that. They read the signs. A country dog knows from the signs when a rabbit has passed by, knows too which way he was heading. Perhaps he has seen a bent weed. London studied Chuck; he made himself an expert on the subject. When Chuck got up from his chair London knew whether he would take up a magazine or go to the kitchen; if it was to be the kitchen, whether he would settle for a drink or open that wonderful refrigerator.

He was even aware that Chuck was going out of his way to avoid people. A dog too hides to lick his wound. He did not mind that they saw little of Helen, the girl downstairs, who for nearly half a year had pampered him. Chuck was all he wanted of companionship.

As time for winter baseball drew near, Chuck's mood blackened. He still dared not let his arm out. In the park with London he could not pitch a ball the way he used to. There came a night when he lay in bed and tried in vain to read.

London whimpered for the light to go out. He did not like any change in their routine. He wanted his usual, "Good night, London."

Down he jumped from his sofa in the front room to walk to the side of the restless man. Chuck would not even look at him. He sniffed. Satisfied that nothing was organically wrong, he went back to curl up on his couch. If London could have put his mind to the problem which overwhelmed Chuck, his answer would have been, why of course Chuck would make a comeback. Any team in the land would be lucky to sign him. Chuck was tops—to London.

The light burned on. Through the archway it kept the dog awake.

Chuck began to fiddle with the radio, listening for sports news, dialing station after station. If he were to give up pitching altogether, could he find a berth as a shortstop? He would make a good shortstop, with a sure hand that could scoop up a grounder and hurl it on its way to first in one continuous motion.

Who would sign him?

Again London stepped lightly across the floor to Chuck's bed. He uttered, yawn-fashion, a distinct, "Ohoo-ahooo." It was a clever trick, done by yawning and stretching at the same time. Chuck was always trying to get him to say something. Even this did not make him look.

Since dog-talk got him nowhere, London struck the side of Chuck's bed with his paw. This was a definite summons. It meant, "I need to go."

Chuck looked at him in disbelief. Not since that first night had the dog asked for this.

Sure now of Chuck's attention, London turned his head significantly toward the switch on the wall. He made his meaning clear. While Chuck lay watching, he crossed the room to stand under the switch. Up on his hind legs he caught at the toggle with front teeth, something he had never tried before.

Off snapped the lights. Off too, on the same connection, faded the radio annoyance. In the sudden blackness the dog waited for his reprimand.

"Okay, you win! Come up here."

With a rush London bounded onto the bed, to push his nose joyously under Chuck's neck.

"You clown!" What chance had worry in the presence of such a spirit? A man's fingers were rubbing the inside of a dog's ears, rubbing his nose, scratching under his jaws. Soon he was able to put it into words.

"You're my bud, London. We'll find a way, huh? Together we'll make it."

The night still held hours for sleep. "Back to bed, old boy. Good night, London."

This was all London had asked for in the first place.

CHAPTER THREE

A Bat in the Face

THE NEW DAY, regardless of the calendar, had to be a holiday.

In the back yard Chuck, perched on a bench, held up a shining metal comb. London needed no coaxing. For half an hour he could be sure of Chuck's undivided attention.

First the comb dragged the loose down gently from the coarse hairs of his coat. Wire teeth brought up the soft brown fuzz. The bristles of the brush made the fur crackle and glisten. Mostly London's coat was dark, with the warm sheen of expensive fur. Brush strokes followed the nap, back and down, back and down.

"Now lie down."

London exposed his belly.

"Come closer."

London got up and lay down again.

Brush, brush, along the light sides of his powerful chest. Here where the hair was longest his fur was marked by the wide bands of creamy white that show in every photograph.

"Leg up."

Brush from chest to paw.

"Now the left. . . . Now get up. . . . Turn around." Brush, brush, inside hind legs. "Higher. I can't reach."

At last the dog was released, to shake his groomed coat, to race in wild circles around the yard. When his nose told of a tennis ball lurking under geraniums he routed it out and thrust it into Chuck's hand.

"Play ball, huh? Okay, but not here. Let's go to the park."

Harvard Park maintains a regulation baseball diamond. In this city playground, now that school had commenced, Chuck and his dog were alone. Chuck stood on the pitcher's mound. As he loosened his pitching arm he did not need marks he had chalked on the backstop to tell him just where the ball passed over the plate. He knew how each pitch should be called, each pitch a little stronger than the one before. Every pitch came back to him in London's mouth.

When he had thrown his quota they strolled across the grass where London was to have his wild runs. The dog was really enjoying himself shagging batted balls.

Chuck decided to play a trick on him.

He tossed the ball as though he would bat out a fly. Instead of knocking it, he caught the ball in his hand. London, who never could wait for the bat to connect, ran out for a head start the moment the ball left Chuck's hand. The crack of bat against ball failed to reach his ears. He searched the air as he ran. How could he have missed this one? He stopped and looked about. With a puzzled expression, he returned to Chuck. The two of them together would have to hunt that ball.

There it was, in Chuck's hand. London sniffed it to make sure there had been no switch.

Chuck laughed.

London didn't find it funny. Anyway he did not like to be laughed at.

Again Chuck was able to fool him, tossing the ball without hitting it. London ran out as before with all his might for a ball that failed to come.

It isn't right to fool him this way, decided Chuck. Next time I'll bat him a good one.

He won't be fooling me again, decided London. Next time he tosses up our ball I'll show him I'm on. I'll take the ball right out of his hand.

So Chuck tossed up the ball.

So London, instead of running out, came up to take the ball lightly in his mouth.

Chuck had started his swing. He could not pull back. A dog's head, a falling ball and a swung bat all sped to a single point in space. The full impact of the bat caught the side of London's head.

A muffled sickening crunch. A dog slumping heavily to the grass. A man on his knees.

Chuck could not even cry out against the thing he had done.

His dog's body twitched under his hands. Was the heart still beating? Were these mere muscle spasms, as of some animal killed for sport?

"Are you all right, boy?"

He saw the bleeding mouth, looked into open glazed eyes. He laid his head on the furry chest to listen, to pray for the heartbeat. There was blood in that open eye, more blood coming from his mouth, and no sign of breathing. All because of a stupid joke! "Are you all right, boy?" Blood in London's unhearing ear.

Nobody was to be seen in this whole playground for him to send for help. Nobody.

Hardly knowing what he was up to, he took the shirt from his back to a faucet and drenched it with cold water. With his wet shirt he wiped London's face. He massaged his legs, afraid to disturb his head.

After what seemed forever, a lapse that might have lasted a quarter of an hour, he went for help. Across the park he ran. Down the street was a drugstore where he could telephone. At the edge of the park he stopped to look back.

London was trying to crawl after him.

London staggered and fell, was up on front feet, dragging himself. As though blind, he veered off in a wrong direction.

"Stay!" Chuck raced toward him. "I'm coming!"

When he reached his side, the dog wagged his tail, not much but the tail did wag. "Try to keep quiet, London." Carefully he got his arm around the dog's legs, cradled him in his arms in an upright position.

"We're going to get you fixed up." Soothing him all the way Chuck carried him to the car.

"Lie still," he begged when London struggled on the yellow leather seat.

In the receiving room of the animal clinic two or three people sitting with their dogs by their sides looked up in surprise at the tall bronzed athlete, naked from the waist up, with a combed-and-brushed shepherd in his arms. The blood on the dog's face was enough to bring the young lady hurrying from behind her desk. "This way." She swung wide a white enameled door.

In an all-white operating room a black poodle stood insolently on the table.

The doctor called in his assistant. "Put her in her cage. Now. Lay him on the table. What hit him?"

"A baseball bat."

London, breathing weakly and in a jerky manner, let the doctor feel his hurt skull. He tried to move as he was told.

"Hope you got the guy who swung on him," said the assistant.

"We were playing ball," said Chuck, but he could not confess how it happened.

After the examination the doctor would only say, "I find no fracture. Young bones are supple." The dog was to be left for observation.

In the small dark hours Chuck was back at the clinic. He knocked at the front door, knocked at the back, and was answered only by the helpless barking of prisoners. His dog was somewhere in there, sick of a concussion, perhaps dying, and no one was on duty. The barking alone was enough to drive him crazy. When, long after dawn, the janitor came, Chuck insisted on paying his bill and having London released. No matter what, so long as London lived he was not going to desert him again.

The first day the sickbed was a bathtub padded with blankets. Leary of any movement, the dog whimpered when he tried to turn his head. Even to move his eyes hurt him. But never a sound of protest came from him when Chuck went over his skull with exploring fingers, searching for the break, the crack he did not find.

Several times Chuck turned him over. In the evening he gathered him up and carried him downstairs. In the back yard London seemed surprised to find that he could stand, with Chuck's help. He looked back to his own raised hind leg as though it were no part of him.

He did not eat or drink.

The second day his eyes cleared. Chuck made his bed on the floor.

At two in the morning of the third day, when Chuck came to turn him, he gave Chuck a look that sent him to the refrigerator.

London could lap warmed milk without moving his jaws.

In a week he walked, though with head cocked over to the left. Within two weeks they could cover a mile, but sometimes Chuck had to carry him home. He still had a faulty sense of balance; he would push into a bush, and Chuck would have to help him out.

In six weeks he was chasing batted balls.

Nearly every day found him and Chuck practicing in Harvard Park. Though it was football season, with basketball, not baseball, in the offing, schoolboys gathered about them. They even got up a sand-lot game on a Saturday, and Chuck would pitch an inning for either side.

During these games London sat behind the mesh backstop, a

tennis ball in his mouth, testing his jaws, waiting for the time when Chuck would play with him alone again. If a boy came to sit with him, it was all right. He was not one of those strictly trained dogs that are never to be touched or spoken to by anyone other than the owners.

If the boy wanted to shake hands, London would look at him gravely. Chuck would call back to them, "Say please, fellow."

"Please, London."

London offered a paw.

"London. Sounds like somebody famous. How come you called him that, Chuck?"

"I was in London once . . ."

Once in London a German V-2 rocket blasted Captain Eisenmann clear through a wall . . .

For three months he had lain in a hospital, trying, on his back, to find out what it was he wanted in this world. Always before he had been too busy to wonder, busy creating a pitching arm. In London he had searched for a larger meaning to life. London to Chuck became a word meaning something more than was reasonably to be expected.

London was the name of his dog years before ever London was born. "London!" Chuck had said to a five-week-old pup. "London. That's your name." He had carried the pup out to the car and placed him on the seat beside him. The infant had sat there, looking out the window, looking at the treetops slipping past. "London." After a while Chuck had said to him, sharply, "London!"

And London had looked up.

"How old is he?" asked the boy who had shaken his paw.

London and Chuck had heard this one before. They were ready with their answer. "Ask him," prompted Chuck.

"How old are you, London?"

London barked once, clearly, then grunted.

"Says he's a little over a year now."

When at last London could take the tennis ball between his jaws and squeeze it flat, he was no longer to be considered on the sick list. His recovery was not yet complete; his head twisted a little to one side as he walked, but Chuck was able to give more attention to his pitching arm.

That arm which through the anxious months had been Chuck's constant worry was, during London's trouble, largely forgotten. London meant more to him than baseball. Perhaps because of this change in emphasis while the two played ball together, the arm responded in a way that delighted his doctor.

"Go ahead and use it now," came the welcome advice.

Well-timed, too, for winter ball was about to begin. For the past three winters Chuck had pitched with the Rosabell Plumbers. The master plumber, who owned the shop and also owned the team, took it for granted that Eisenmann would be one of his two pitchers again, sharing the mound chores for fifty dollars a Sunday. It had to be a Sunday, because most of the men on the team held weekday jobs. Only the two pitchers were paid; the other players were, in theory at least, employees of the shop. Actually half a dozen of them had served time with the majors, and the Plumbers as a team were good enough to beat the best in the land.

Chuck would not take London with him onto the diamond. He was not that sure of himself. After they drove together to Pasadena, he left his dog in the Arroyo Seco parking lot to guard the yellow convertible. When his teammates saw Chuck of the Chisox in his older San Diego Padres' uniform, he came in for some ribbing, but found he could laugh with them.

Sunday baseball with the Plumbers was a pleasure unmarred by the day-after-day-and-under-the-lights-too bickering that soured life with the Sox, where each new day came too soon to erase the ill will of the day before. These men played ball for the joy of the game. When Sundays rolled around, everybody on the Rosabell team was looking forward to seeing everybody else. Chuck pitched his half games, and went back to his dog, and his comeback went off so well that an item in the St. Louis *Sporting News* reported it.

This meant a lot to a pitcher without a commitment. Scouts were about, hunting talent for spring rosters.

Prospects were picking up for Chuck, and for London.

CHAPTER FOUR

London Gets His Contract

EVERYWHERE the feel of baseball was in the air. Though it was not yet spring, schoolboys who had been quietly playing catch in side streets began to move openly into Harvard Park for sand-lot games. Since London did not go with Chuck into the dugout at Pasadena, here was a chance to acquaint the dog with the game and teach him the fine points.

"How much do you boys know about baseball bats?"

Carefully Chuck laid out on the grass the bats he kept in his car, while London and four of the boys attended. One bat was his heaviest, his thirty-six-inch Lou Gehrig, thin-handled but heavy on the slugging end. Next to it he laid his slender outfield fungo. Last was Chuck's favorite, his thirty-five-inch Jackie Robinson with the thick handle. In competition this bottle-bat helped him maintain a batting average well above that of most pitchers.

"Watch, boys." He picked up the heaviest, the Lou Gehrig, and swatted out a long fly for London. While the dog was galloping out for it, he explained, "Strictly a home-run bat. Too heavy for practice." He laid the Lou Gehrig with the others. Back trotted London with the ball, his head still a little awry.

"London, when we finish this lesson on bats, we'll have a game of pepper. For pepper the right bat is a fungo. Fungo is a word which has to do with batting a ball in practice. Will you bring me my *fungo* bat, please?"

London looked at him and wagged his tail. He did like to be included in the talk, but he was not sure what was being said to him. He waited for more.

"Don't you know what a fungo is?" The question was aimed at all five students. "Come now, London, do you mean I have to get up and go over there and show it to you? Bring the fungo bat to me."

Here was a direct command. London had to act on it. He had his key word, *bat*. Chuck wanted a bat. He nosed the bats lying there and closed his jaws on the one Chuck had just used, the heavy Lou Gehrig. He mouthed it a little way in from the handle. When he lifted, the heavy end dragged.

"Seems to me you've got a mouthful," Chuck protested. "You picked the heaviest one of all! I asked you to bring me my fungo."

Down went London's tail. If the words did not all register, there was no escaping the thought. Out of his mouth fell the rejected bat. It hit a paw. He held up his paw for sympathy. "Ooo! Oooo!" The boys laughed. He could be a real ham when he had an audience.

"Don't bring us your troubles. You're not hurt. And I still don't have my fungo."

These boys owned dogs, or hoped to. Down on their knees by the bats they missed neither word nor movement. As London pawed at the bats, they were watching a dog's mind and a man's mind working together. London gave the Jackie Robinson a push with his nose and passed on to the other. Here was a toothpick of a bat, the one most unlike his first choice. When he took it lightly into his mouth, Chuck encouraged him. "There's a difference, London, isn't there? Long and slim." London's tail came up. His jaws slid along the fungo's narrow shaft till he found the balance. Up came his head. Bat held high he strutted to Chuck.

"Atta boy, Lon. Hand it to me. Here's the one to bat out balls. This is a fungo. Remember, *fungo*. Pass it along, boys. The slender fungo, easy for batting out flies, is not to be used in a game. A hard-pitched ball would shatter it. London, there's a bat over there we haven't talked about. Bring it to me, please. Bring me my favorite now, my Jackie Robinson."

London looked thoughtfully at Chuck a moment, then turned to the boys as though to ask, "Do you know what he means?" When he went to the bats he did choose the thirty-five incher. But the Jackie Robinson was thick at the handle; his jaws would not slide up the increasing thickness. He had to seize it near center, and it was all he could do to carry it.

"How does he know to do this?" asked a boy.

"Keep watching," said Chuck. "Now look at this bat. See how thick the handle is? Here's something to hold on to. This is the bat I like to start out with. Not everybody likes a Jackie Robinson; you have to find the one that fits your grip. Now look at the swatting end. Here you see the trade-mark burned into the wood. Whenever you pick up a bat, always look for the trade-mark. The trade-mark indicates the flow of the grain. When you bat a ball, keep the trade-mark up. If you bat with the trade-mark toward the pitch, the bat may snap at the handle. All right, London, care to join us in a game of pepper?"

London did indeed care to.

"Then bring me my fungo, please."

London now had the key word, fungo, to go with pepper games.

Chuck took his stand and began swinging the fungo bat. Four boys lined up on the grass before him. In the middle of the line they made a place for London. Each of these five in line faced the batter, each the same distance from him. The boy at the end of the line tossed a baseball to Chuck, who batted it lightly to the next in line, who again threw to Chuck. Now London was next, so Chuck sliced one with the proper English, and the dog took the bounce easily into his mouth. London placed the ball in the next boy's hand to let him throw it back so he would not have to get out of line.

After the game, "Gosh he's smart!" the boys decided.

Chuck said, "He's going to be the smartest dog in the world." He knew this was true. "You'll never be able to fool him about a fungo again."

"Let's try him," someone suggested.

Chuck switched the bats around on the grass.

"Now, London, we'll see if you can bring me the fungo."

London brought it without hesitation.

"I get it," said one of the boys. "It's the bat you've been using with us. He smells you on it."

Chuck looked at him a moment. "All right. Put it back with the others. Mix them up." The boy did.

"London."

London was ready!

"London, please bring me that bottle-bat, the one with the thick handle. You know, the one I said was my favorite. Bring me the Jackie Robinson."

Obviously this was not what he had expected to hear. Perhaps it was chance, but the bat he took hold of, after pawing them over, was the very bat Chuck had asked for. Finding it heavy for his tiring jaws, he dragged it across the grass and placed the handle in Chuck's outstretched hands.

The boys would believe anything of him now. Chuck's teachings made an impression, but they would never forget the dog.

When spring training began the San Francisco Seals bid for Chuck, and he turned them down. It was a firm offer, promising even his full Chicago salary. The club could afford this because Chuck held his own pink slip, which meant a chance to put a big-league pitcher on the roster without paying a big-league purchase price. He turned them down because the dog would not be permitted on the long road trips up and down the coast. He had given London his promise.

There would always be other work, even if he had to enter an umpire's school.

At last, well on into May, a long distance call came from the little city of Kearney, Nebraska, asking if Chuck would pitch with the Kearney Irishmen. Before the conversation ended, Chuck had committed himself and London to a verbal agreement.

"You will be written into our contract, London," Chuck was able to tell him. "It means less money, but you are party to this deal."

Everything they owned was loaded into the automobile. Top down, they climbed out of the wide valley that contains Greater Los Angeles, and for the tenth time Chuck went over details. "You are to live with me. You are to ride with me, to and from games, in our own conveyance. Gas paid. That's what the man said."

London, sitting tall at his side, gazed at him in admiration.

Every mountain slope, every bird in the sky, added to their adventure. On the other side of the San Gabriel Mountains the highway drops to irrigated land. Here along the Mojave River they skirted a wide area of green grass fenced in with barbed wire. "Like the country we're headed for," Chuck exulted.

To help London with their conversation Chuck now and then emphasized new words. Like tractor. "Look over there. That's a tractor." London observed the tractor. Since Chuck, who once was a farm boy, had pointed out a tractor before, he already knew *tractor.* He did not find it necessary to respond. Only when a meaning was unclear would he look to Chuck for help.

Chuck said, "That's a locomotive." He often said things which the dog could tell, from the way they were said, he was supposed to understand yet he did not. Then he would turn to the man with a question in his clear brown eyes. For instance, "That's a locomotive." Chuck did like big words.

Locomotive London did not recall ever having heard before. He looked at the man as they drove along the broad open road, then turned to gaze at a freight train laboring up the grade.

"The locomotive," answered Chuck, recognizing the question, "is pulling boxcars."

Boxcar was definitely part of his vocabulary. On their way to Sunday ball in Pasadena a long train of empties had blocked the way. Chuck had told him, during the wait at the railroad crossing, "That's a boxcar." The train was in no hurry and neither were they. "That's a boxcar. Another boxcar." Boxcars rumbled slowly past. If Chuck had started at the beginning he would have kept count. He switched off the ignition. "Boxcar." London liked his lessons in language. "Boxcar. Boxcar."

In the desert he advanced from *boxcar* to *locomotive*. Chuck said, "The locomotive is pulling boxcars." He believed his dog capable of taking *boxcars* from the sentence and having *locomotive* left. It was the way Chuck himself had picked up French in the Army. Because he had a few words to start with, when mouthfuls of French were jabbered at him, he rapidly caught onto more. Why could not London do the same? He had a brain.

Chuck made a point of not overdoing key words, careful not to say the same thing always in the same way. A child does not learn English through hearing simple barked-out commands, always word for word: "Lie down! Give me your paw! Come here! Heel!" The last thing he wanted was a well-trained automaton incapable of responding to the new and unrehearsed. His dog would learn English as a person learns it. Even when a human is too young to know that a sentence must have a noun for a subject, a verb for its predicate, and may or may not have an object, his parent talks to him in sentences. Before he can know a single letter of the twenty-six in the alphabet, he can make up long paragraphs that can be diagramed. Surely London would do the same, if only lips and tongue would shape the sounds for him. His ears and his mind were as keen as those of any child of ten.

The next time London saw a train, laboring its way toward the Continental Divide, and Chuck referred to the engine as a locomotive, London did not turn to the man for enlightenment. He could be most nonchalant over anything he already knew.

"The locomotive gives off smoke."

London knew smoke. Smoke came from Helen's father's mouth. Chuck and London did not like smoke; smoke made London sneeze. Attentively he observed the smoke trail behind the locomotive.

Sometimes it was London who pointed out the sights. In the

foothills of the Rockies a jack rabbit bounded across the pavement. London struck Chuck's shoulder and whimpered.

"Okay, boy. I see him. Bigger than a cottontail, isn't he?"

Or a buzzard sailing the sky. London saw it first. He had to share the sight with Chuck.

Once in the high country of northern New Mexico a mountain coyote stood silently regarding their car as it invaded his territory. A wild coyote shows little fear of a moving automobile, even though the top is down, exposing the occupants. London, not permitted to bark while the car was in motion, uttered a strangled cry, licked Chuck's ear, and flung himself back to lean out.

How it must hurt not to be able to put thoughts into words! As the car passed, the noble animal stood at the side of the road, as tall as London, with a bushy tail, totally unlike those bedraggled specimens slinking back and forth in stinking cages.

While London gazed back, Chuck, keeping his eyes on the rear-view mirror, saw another coyote come to stand beside its mate. Shoulder to shoulder, a pair of coyotes. Without London's keen eyes he would have missed an unforgettable sight.

A mile a minute across the face of America, these travelers did not always have to talk. Their silences were unlike those yawning gaps that separate people weary of being tied together. Without words they made their understanding known. Boundless was London's agreement when Chuck did break the silence.

"Those willows along that stream! There's the place where hunting would be good. I bet you'd find your rabbit there quick enough. What do you say, London?"

At times Chuck's thoughts took form beyond the dog's experience. "A thousand a month, London. I know Kearney's not big time, but, all things considered, this is a good contract. I have a feeling it is leading to something big. Something more than baseball altogether, and it has to do with you. London, you bring me luck. After the game's won and the stadium's empty, we'll be on our way."

London's eyes said, "How wonderful you are. So smart."

Nobody could accuse Chuck of talking to himself. He would not have spoken had not London been listening. London drew his thoughts beyond his little world of baseball. The dog brought him a wider vision.

Six days they were on the road, and on the seventh they pulled into Kearney, on a Sunday afternoon in May. This did not mean they were cutting it fine. Baseball players sometimes jump off a bus directly into a game.

It was four o'clock. The game, under the lights, was scheduled for eight. Chuck hunted up the manager.

"When did you pitch last?" The man, who had never met Chuck, knew his history through baseball's record books.

"Nine, maybe ten days ago. An All-Star game against U.C.L.A."

"Can you throw a few innings tonight? Our people would like to see it."

"I'm ready." En route he had bounced baseballs off concrete curbs at motels while London retrieved. He had thrown countless rocks at mountainsides. His pitching arm felt good.

The manager gave him a copy of the contract. From a carbon he read aloud, " 'In addition said player will be permitted to convey his German shepherd dog on all road trips in his own conveyance.' " He laughed. "A clause to make baseball history. When do we see this famous dog?"

"You'll meet him tonight. He'll be on the field."

CHAPTER FIVE

London Meets the Team

THE CLUB would naturally be expecting its star pitcher to pull rank. If only Chuck could make it free and easy, as it had been with the Rosabell team. Instead he found himself dredging up memories from Chicago which he would prefer to have left undisturbed.

He didn't have to worry over what he would eat for supper. Even when he was sure of himself he would not eat after three o'clock if he was scheduled to pitch under the lights. His problem was how he would make out with his new teammates. Or rather, now that he had committed himself to Manager Stickney, how he and London would make out tonight. Never until now had he been ready to take London along with him into a stadium.

Thoughts of the impending encounter bothered London not at all. In their motel he downed full rations.

After a try at a nap Chuck got into his new uniform. It fit him. Thirty-six with a forty-eight blouse.

To London Chuck's uniform meant a long wait in a parked car. At the parking lot he could hardly believe his ears when Chuck asked,

"Want to come along?"

Kearney's Memorial Stadium is an imposing pile of concrete. The main entrance tops the concrete bowl. Up here, through twin gates above long tiers of seats, players and spectators alike must pass. Though the sun was still above the western horizon, a few dyed-in-the-wool fans were already in their places.

"Here he comes!" called out one of the early birds. "With his Seeing Eye dog!" It's the kind of razzing to keep a ballplayer on an even keel.

The ex-Chicago pitcher, with Kearney's label on him now, swung down the wide-tread steps of Kearney's stadium, a big man with his head high, his spikes dangling from his right hand. The spectacular dog at his left carried his two gloves. Down the long center aisle they made their entry, and he kept up a steady bluff of talk directed only to the dog.

The assembled team, perhaps eighteen men, was already on the field. Pepper games were in progress on the grass between home plate and the wire, and along the coaching lines. IRISHMEN spelled out green letters across each zipped-up shirt front, matching the label on Chuck's chest. 1, 12, 6, 26, and so on, green numerals on shirt backs, identified the individual players.

It was for the most part an older group, with only a sprinkling of youth. These men lacked the slick close-knit flair of the Sox. That was reassuring. Less drill promised more fun. The ragged appearance of the team was in part due to the way sleeves of sweat shirts showed below the blouses. A rainbow of sleeves! Red, some blue, yellow, green, carefree colors after Chicago's uniform black. An older player here and there was noticeably overweight. The manager had said the group was not well-acquainted—Chuck told himself again he had nothing to worry about—and they had had very little spring training. He watched an easy hopper slip between a player's legs.

At the bottom of the aisle, where boxes would someday be when this ambitious new stadium was complete, Chuck hunted for a gate to the field. He could see through the wire backstop how the players were keenly aware of the approach of their new pitcher, and of the German shepherd at his side.

"Over here, Eisenmann!"

London was really keyed up. Though he had never before seen the inside of a stadium, he did know a baseball diamond. The geometry of baseball is everywhere the same, down to the last half inch. Only the stands and the fences and the gates vary. "And," Chuck could have explained to him, "the hardness of the ground." That makes a difference.

The hinged gate was made of pipe; below it five concrete steps led down to the grass. Chuck propped it open and, with a signal of his hand, had London sit atop these steps while he went down to encounter the team.

"Men," introduced their manager, "this is Chuck Eisenmann. Meet our right-handed pitcher." So there was not to be a lot of names. Probably the manager could not yet call them all off if he tried. Chuck kept his mind on what he planned to do next.

"Hi, fellows," he grinned and waved.

Luck was with him. One of the boys was holding in his hand a Jackie Robinson—there was no mistaking that thick-handled bat. If only he would hold onto that bat, it would give London a chance to perform something over and above his usual routine. The bat was of the right length too. Not likely would this outfit own more than one bottle-bat of this particular model. Bats were strewn on the grass. A dozen more waited in the rack. As for London, he sat alert atop the concrete steps, the two gloves hanging from his mouth, impatient for his cue to come and take the spotlight.

First Chuck had to set the stage. He sat down and began putting on his spikes. "When do we hit?" he called out. Everybody must be made to think about bats.

"You pitchers," laughed Manager Stickney. "Always afraid you'll never get your hands on a bat. We were just getting ready. Eisenmann, you start it off."

"London!" Chuck was tying his shoelace. With two bounds London cleared the steps and was at his side. "Would you mind"—Chuck had to make himself keep the excitement out of his voice—"my gloves, please." As he stood, London pushed them into his hand. "Thank you." Now he was sure of their undivided attention.

"London, would you be so kind as to bring me a bat?"

London gave Chuck the sly look of a conspirator. Instead of stepping immediately to the bats on the ground, he was deliberately stretching out the interval between a command and his performance. He was already enough of a showman to relish the moment, with an eye to the onlookers. A bat? Easy! He walked over to paw at the first bat he came to, found the balance and hoisted it clear of the ground.

"What d'you know!" exclaimed one of the men. Bat in mouth London gave him a bored look.

Instead of taking the offered bat from him, Chuck turned on a heel and walked away. As he sauntered the few steps to home plate, he too was trying to take it easy, to pretend they were not acting at all. He did not have to look back to know that London would be strutting after him, bat in mouth.

At home plate he sailed one of his two gloves carelessly toward the dugout and stuffed the other in his pocket. "Thank you, London." He took the bat from his dog's jaws.

Even if the rest of the scene failed to come off, to the men what had already happened was obviously enough. He gripped the bat and swished the air. Everything was going to be all right. He looked at the bat in pretended disgust. Flinging it away, he summoned his dog.

"London." The fans up above were watching as intently as his teammates. He had to talk loudly to include everybody. "London, you know I no longer start out practice with one of those thin-handled jobs." If he said it slowly, too, it would suggest that London was hanging on his every word. "Bring me, if you will, my usual. Bring me a thirty-five-inch Jackie Robinson." And he prayed that his dog would not be able to find it, either back there on the ground or in the rack; and as he prayed he kept his eye on the man who was holding onto the bat he had asked for.

London held his ears stiff and alert. He was actually playing out his part here before a crowd better than if they had been at home in their own back yard practicing. This dog belonged to the theater! Not a sound came from his audience. Chuck, delighted at the way London was apparently thinking it all over carefully, could not help laying it on thicker. "Or," he went on, "maybe a thirty-five-inch Ted Kluszewski."

Ted Kluszewski. London had never before heard such a word, and Chuck knew it. He gave Chuck the look, a sort of raised eyebrow we-know-something-they-don't-know look. Then he proceeded to do as he was told.

"*Bring me... bring me ...*" Those were words that mattered. London stood by the bats on the ground. "*Jackie Robinson.*" Words to hold on to. His jaws well remembered the peculiar thickening of a bat handle. His paw could find no bat on the ground with a Jackie Robinson handle. As though deep in thought he rejected them one by one. With never a self-conscious glance at any of the men who gathered about him in admiration, he left the bats on the ground to step briskly up to the bat rack. The rack was much like the one he knew at Harvard Park. He noted each handle. And all the time Chuck was watching one man only, the fellow who still held onto the Jackie Robinson bat, afraid he would put a premature end to the performance by offering his bat to the dog.

When London failed to find the single object he had been asked to bring, in the places where it ought to be, he ran back to Chuck for further instructions.

Chuck laughed and rubbed his dog's head. "I know your trouble, old boy! You're just a softie. London, you are actually bashful! Well, here in Kearney you're among friends now. You say one of the boys already has my bat? Don't let that stop you. *Take it away from him!* Get me my bat."

Again the dog added to the suspense by delaying, as though working out in his mind a complicated order. Actually this too was simple. The bat order was still valid; the only thing Chuck had added was not hard: "*. . . one of the boys . . .*" He had his clue, and he had his new stimulus: "*Get me my bat.*" The rest of the talk could just as well have been in German—or Hottentot. He stood there so long that Chuck was about to frame a new sentence with the words *Jackie Robinson* in it when London started off.

Four of the spellbound players were holding bats in their hands. London stepped up to one of them—only to pass him by.

The second bat-holder tried to help out by giving his bat to the dog. London took it from him, for politeness only. The handle was thin. He dropped it to the ground.

As he neared the third man his tail began to wave in the air. Before his mouth touched the bat in the man's grip everybody could see what was taking place. And Chuck was holding his breath.

London mouthed the handle. He challenged the bat-holder by taking the slugging end into his jaws. The man let go. The heavy bat twisted out of the dog's mouth and fell.

London looked up. "You hurt my teeth!" he objected in pantomime. Then he pawed the bat on the grass.

He knew where to find the balance. His jaws closed at the fulcrum. Up came his proud head. Up his tail. He carried the bat to Chuck on the double, as though to a triumphant roll of drums.

It is doubtful how much attention was being accorded Chuck and his denouement. He was holding the bat up in the air as though it were a telescope. To make sure that he held what he wanted, he pretended to read what was on the handle. But the people were aglow with magic they had already witnessed, right there before their eyes.

They did, however, listen as he read aloud, for all to hear:

" 'Louisville Slugger. Jackie Robinson model. Thirty-five inches.' That's my boy, London. I thank you."

Players crowded around the dog.

"Will you shake hands?" one asked London.

London would not even look at him.

Another player tried to explain this way. "No, gosh no, that's not how you ask a dog. You're supposed to say, 'Give me a paw.' Watch me. Hey, London, give me your paw."

London would give him neither a paw nor a look.

"Why won't he shake hands with us, Eisenmann?"

Chuck smiled. "Did you say, 'Please'?"

So the man did say please.

So London shook hands. And he wagged a friendly tail.

Every Irishman had to shake hands with London. And shake with Chuck too.

CHAPTER SIX

Play Ball

THE MAN who goes to a ball game for the fun of it is not one of the paid players. The team sees baseball as a business proposition. Its most loyal star turns his back on his mates when he finds he can get more money somewhere else. It's cold business with the owner too. He'll sell his best man when the price is right. For the most part the management's shrewd eye is on the man who goes to a ball game for the fun of it.

From the start of the season, baseball at Kearney showed signs of drawing paying customers who did not care much for the game itself. Among the crowds passing through the turnstiles were many who wanted to see the dog. Farmers drove in with their families from far back in the sand hills because the word had gotten around that the Irishmen had a dog on the team who actually knew baseball.

The home team was in uniform and on the field at six. The stands were brightly sprinkled with people as early as a quarter after six, for a game that would not begin until eight. The advent of London was the only way the club could account for this.

At seven the visiting team took over. Not until eight would the "Star Spangled Banner" signal the opening of the contest. But at any time from six o'clock on, spectators could count on seeing something of London.

Recognizing a box-office gimmick, Manager Stickney persuaded Chuck to work up a routine of clever tricks for London's admirers. So, when pepper games were forming, Pitcher Eisenmann and his dog could be seen trotting around the outfield, putting on a sideshow. The dog halted at the foul line while the man ran ahead and leaned over. London cleared his back in a flying leap. Or he would jump through Chuck's circled arms. On another approach London landed on the man's back and rode him.

The tricks were good, but many a circus dog does tricks. The people made it clear they wanted to see the dog play baseball.

An ordinary game of pepper, with London in the line-up, proved a real drawing card. As soon as Chuck played catch with a teammate or with a ball boy, the fans filtered into the nearest seats. Here they would soon see London in a game of pepper.

Half a dozen town boys mingled with the players on that generous fifty-foot-wide strip of grass between backstop and the stands. These teen-age amateurs were the ball boys and the bat boys. They shagged balls and generally made themselves useful. The most expert among them got to play a little catch with their heroes.

Chuck tossed them a few. Then he sent London for his fungo bat. Now came the rush of kids, each bidding for a chance to stand in line with London. Chuck waved all aside to bat a few for his dog.

It does not seem possible that a dog can catch a batted ball without injuring his teeth. A regulation baseball is hard. The batter has to know just how to slice it. Only Chuck and nobody else, ever, was allowed to hit a grounder for London's jaws. Chuck could slice a backspin, with English on the ball to make it rise softly from the bounce, whereupon London would take it easily into his mouth. It did not look easy from the grandstand, though.

Now London was ready for pepper. Two Irishmen were in the line-up, and three of the little-leaguers. The dog's place was in the middle of the line. Men, boys, and dog, each stood at arm's length from the next in line, and all faced the batter.

The man on the left threw the ball to Chuck. Crack! Chuck lined it sharply to a little-leaguer. The boy caught it neatly and threw it to the batter. This time Chuck sliced his backspin for his dog. London could catch a bounce high or low or scrape a ball off the ground; he laid the caught ball in the mitt of the man next in line. This was Ray Johnson, outfielder, who had to throw Chuck the ball he himself was to receive.

When the batted ball came back, London hogged Johnson's catch knowing how he delighted his claque whenever he ad-libbed.

"London," called Chuck. "Was that *your* ball?"

With a sidelong glance at Johnson London turned the question over to him.

"Well," replied the outfielder, playing up to the dog, "it was sort of between us."

London gave him the ball. Johnson threw, and Chuck batted to him again. He was laughing and he let the grounder go between his legs. So the ball once more was London's; he shagged it and placed it safely in Johnson's hand.

The stands missed none of this. "Hey, Johnson, give him your place in the outfield too."

Batting practice followed pepper games. Batting practice might be likened to a dry-run of the game. In it the team works together as a unit. This was London's cue to subside behind the wire.

That did not mean that he went off duty. He was a work dog, and baseball was his work. In the wild, he could have been a relentless leader of the hunt; or as a blind man's guide have carried an afflicted human into the world of light. As Chuck's helper he kept himself alert to the players, whether the ball was in practice or in play, quick to learn the game, fathoming the plays, watching for his chance to take part.

A foul was ticked into the stands. The dog was after it almost before a fan caught it. Had a game been in progress London would have waited for express permission before entering the stands. He knew this ball was not in play. He raced up the concrete aisle, a ball boy and a uniformed cop not far behind.

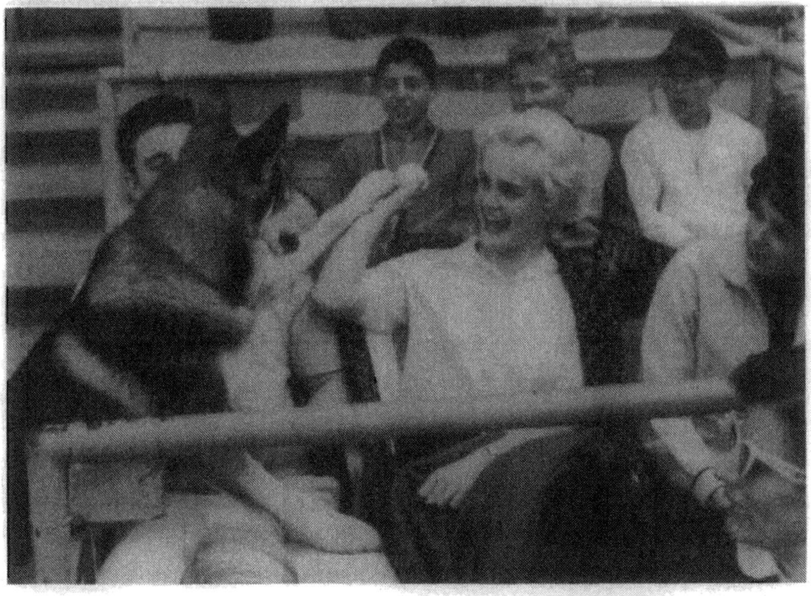

Baseball at Kearney differed from ball in a big-league park in this minor respect: here that ball was still claimed by the management, regardless of what fan was able to get his hooks on it. Before the time of London, however, boys and cops had a time of it, trying to enforce the claim.

Into the proper row ran the dog, pushing past knees. There was no ball to be seen, and no one to give the culprit away, but a dog's nose was able to tell when he reached a man with the ball in his pocket. It would be bad form to threaten force to get it back, so London merely stared the man down until in embarrassment he had to fish the ball out of his pocket. Nor would London let him throw it back over the wire to its rightful owners; he blocked the pitch, determined that the ball was his, to be surrendered only to him, his until he could turn it over to the cop.

After Kearney's batting practice the limelight shifted to the

Plainsmen. These men who poured out of the visitors' dugout were not labeled *Plainsmen;* their road uniforms proclaimed *North Platte,* following the custom whereby the Irishmen, too, wore uniforms to advertise their home town when they played away from home. The visitors from North Platte were good men, perhaps the best in the league, though the second-place Irishmen were breathing down their necks.

Although North Platte had taken over, there still remained, away down left-field foul line in this spacious park, a strip of grass between foul line and fence. Here Chuck and London and a group of London's juvenile admirers relaxed. Boys are endlessly eager to know how to teach a dog.

At seven-thirty North Platte vacated the field. Now each team in turn had fifteen minutes for infield practice. After the Irishmen, and then the Plainsmen, Chuck, without his dog, warmed up on the side lines. He pitched over thirty slow lobs to his catcher. A few breaking balls. A few fork balls. A few change-of-paces. That arm of his was under good control; he was pitching every third or fourth day, and sometimes the whole game through; in Kearney he had found a doctor who really understood.

Still, when he was about to pitch in competition, he was never able to take it easy. Call it stage fright if you will, but as the time drew near for him to step to the mound, he was anxious and restless.

"What time is it, Jerry?"

At the sound of Chuck's keyed-up voice London jumped to his feet.

Jerry yelled from the dugout, "You've got three minutes, Chuck."

London decided Chuck needed him.

Chuck stopped him in his tracks. "Anybody talking to you?"

Down went the tail, and back the dog, to wait behind his protection.

Chuck was really bearing down on his pitches when the loudspeaker gave warning. He beckoned his dog to his side, and just in time, for over the public address system blared the opening notes of the national anthem.

Oh, say can you see! Stand up, stand up, wherever you are. A man with a cap places his cap over his heart. A dog needs a hand signal from his owner, to sit, not stand, at attention, and show his respect in the proud way he holds his head, listening to the music.

This song so regularly opens a game of ball that it is said a visiting Englishman was led to believe the last two words of the "Star Spangled Banner" were "Play ball!"

The Irishmen are in place.

Now from their dugout the Plainsmen set up their steady jeering in an attempt to upset a temperamental pitcher. No wonder. They still smart from their last encounter with Chuck on the mound. He shut them out. One to nothing. And in ten innings.

Chuck is busy digging himself a little hole on the mound. With his spikes he digs in the clay in front of the rubber. He takes his time about it too. Digging his toe hold.

"Aw, Ump! Make him throw!"

"Hope everybody brought lunch," a foghorn voice boomed. "Speedball Eisenmann! Yeah, a three-hour game!"

Ball one.

"Blowed up already!" howls the delighted enemy. "Hey, Stickney, better get Sajevic hot in the bull pen!"

London is irked, even if Chuck is not. Though he knows barkers don't bite, he can't keep the hair from rising a little. He stays behind the wire, out of the range of dangerous line drives, but ready for action if Chuck should need him.

Pitcher Chuck is having trouble with wet fingers.

"London, please," he calls. "The rosin bag!"

Over there, at the base of the concrete, stands the stiff canvas ball bag. London sticks in his nose to rummage among the balls until he comes upon the gritty little rosin sack. Because he dislikes rosin on his teeth he draws it out gingerly and hurries with it to the mound.

When Chuck succeeds in retiring the side, no hit, no score, out races the dog to greet this greatest of all pitchers, reaching him near third-base foul line. He takes Chuck's glove. He fusses over him a little before walking proudly back at his side.

With the Irishmen at bat the dog acts as a charm. He sits at the far end of the dugout. Whoever touches him on his way to the plate will have luck with him as he swings. Each batter leaving the dugout places his hand on London's head. If London were to be absent he would not step out so sure of himself, so confident of his ability to hit. But London is not absent.

Nevertheless, in the bottom of the second, Ray Johnson, the outfielder, forgets the ritual. He reaches the plate without having placed a hand on the team mascot. He misses a ball in his power. Strike! It happens that Ray Johnson is the league's home-run leader. He calls time, runs back to stroke London's head. On the next pitch Johnson clouts his homer.

The third inning finds Chuck at bat. He too has stroked the dog's head en route. Chuck waits till the pitch is right, then lines his favorite handle-hit into short center field. Chuck is on first.

The first-base coach never asks this pitcher, "Want your jacket?" With Chuck's precious elbow in active service, the jacket is routine. That pitching arm must not cool off while Chuck waits around on base.

The umpire holds up both hands.

"Time!"

Time for London to snap Chuck's blue windbreaker from the top of the dugout and race with it across the heart of the infield with all possible speed. A steady clapping sets up for him in the stands. Halfway out, a dragging sleeve trips him. He drops the garment, picks it up again and charges the rest of the way.

"Thank you, London."

The umpire permits the dog on the diamond while he is officiating. Certainly less time is taken out for London to bring the warmup jacket, than would be needed by the nimblest bat boy.

Nor do the Plainsmen object. Good crowd reaction means money for all.

The stands give London a hand as he lopes back to the dugout.

The fifth inning also brings special work for the team's mascot. Chuck pitches a ball a fraction higher than he intended. Too late to call it back! The batter shifts his weight, an eager light in his eye. He swings. Crack! It's a round trip! A two-run homer hit off Chuck. The ball clears the fence just inside the foul-line marker, but not before London is off on a tear.

Away out there beyond the fence, outside the park altogether, sit about fifteen boys, free-loaders watching the game from the side of the hill. As London runs he sizes them up. They have a seventy-five yard head start on him. Every ounce of his strength goes into his handicap race.

"There goes your ball game, Chuck," sings out a Plainsman. That homer has set the game two to one in their favor.

A distant gate with rusty hinges does not stop this dog. If before his teeth can close upon the ball, any one of the boys out there finds it and can return it to the dugout despite the threat of the dog at his side, that boy will have his choice: seventy-five cents or a free admission. To London it means more.

In the shadows from the outfield light, his nose locates the ball. He is back in the park before a new ball is out of the umpire's pocket. With a glance to the mound for Chuck's approval, he races past the dugout, careful not to set foot on the skinned diamond, then home to place the ball in the umpire's hand.

Now the umpire has to say it.

"Thank you, London."

When he finds that London has not slobbered on the ball, he puts it back into play.

Many a ball has London saved from outer space. It must be admitted that some he retrieved belonged to other teams. Because of London, the Kearney ball bag holds a sprinkling of Goldsmiths and Spauldings, though the club buys only Wilsons.

London did his best to comfort Chuck in the dugout after Chuck let a homer be hit off him.

At the close of the inning London also saves the club a bat. An Irishman connects, and flings his bat aside in such a careless manner that the bat lands midway between home plate and the visitor's dugout. The runner is tagged, retiring the side. As the Plainsmen come in, one of them picks up this Kearney bat to carry it with him to his own stack.

One thing Chuck never had to teach London was his keen sense of property. The dog races to the visitor to correct his error and take the bat away from him.

"Buy your own!" calls out a hep fan. "Good boy, London!"

In the sixth, the seventh, and the top of the eighth, the Plainsmen go down in order, eight via the strike-out route. The only hit off Chuck in all eight innings is that homer by Callahan. But good pitching cannot change the score, not without runs. Two to one for their side. Two runs against Chuck.

Pitching against him is Wells. Wells is good. Tonight he leads Chuck two-to-one going into the last half of the eighth.

Wells has two out. Suddenly a boot by the third baseman and one of Wells's rare passes put two on.

And Chuck is up!

"Hey, Floyd," pleads a voice from above, "give us a pinch hitter!" For Chuck is a pitcher, and a pitcher notoriously cannot hit.

The Irishmen stick with Chuck.

Two out. A man on first. A man on second. The game at stake. The Irishmen's tying run is on second; their winning run waits on first. And their pitcher is at bat.

Chuck chooses a Ted Kluszewski of his favorite length, thirty-five inches, and moves up on the handle. He considers Wells a cutie.

The Plainsmen hurler works the count to two balls, two strikes, with Chuck getting only a piece of his second strike. Reading Wells's mind, Chuck figures a slider is coming, a cheap curve, a nickel curve that does not break as much as a batter is led to expect. At the end of Wells's windup, Chuck suddenly steps forward for his swing. The slider does come. The ball is in his power. With hands well up on the bat, à la Pepper Martin, it will not get past him. Inside. Belt high. Exactly what he expected.

A snap of the wrist drives the ball sharply between left and center fielders. Chuck is all the way to second base before the relay man can return it to the infield.

Two runs have crossed the plate.

The score?

Three to two!

So it stands at the first half of the ninth.

Chuck has pitched a crucial game without relief. His elbow is tiring. Right away he walks two batters, placing his lead in jeopardy. He no longer snaps them out. Two on! Chuck is responsible for putting North Platte's winning run on first.

A gambler in the stands, not much of a sport, with maybe five dollars at stake, sets up a steady, "Get him out! He's washed up! Get him out! He's washed up!"

"Aw, shut up," yells his neighbor. "He'll do okay."

Stickney is not so sure. He's got the reliefer throwing in the bull pen. "Time," say Stickney. The umpire verifies with upheld arms.

There's a meeting on the mound. "I still got it in me." Chuck wants to go the distance; he is able to share his confidence with manager and with catcher. "I'll get 'em out. Let's go."

His next pitch is lined up by the batter into a double play. "Atta boy, Chuck," yells the same gambler who had wanted his throat cut.

Before the last bat in this ball game swings, the catcher hollers from behind the plate, "Hey, Chuck! Keep it high! He's strictly a low-ball hitter!"

Chuck nods solemnly. He takes from his catcher the fast-ball sign, fires it chest high on the handle. The ball hits the bat rather than the batter hitting the ball. An easy pop up to the mound!

In his mitt Chuck holds the ball that ended the game.

Don't think our dog does not know the score. He has been on his feet since that meeting on the mound. He is first to charge the field, to rush Chuck, jump all over him, lick his face, grab away his glove, while teammates wait their turn to shake their pitcher's hand.

In the happy crowd that should be taking off for home, many wait for a closer look at the dog. They know that when Chuck gets his cleats off he and London will walk among them.

CHAPTER SEVEN

Rhubarb

LIFE FOR Chuck and London was not all baseball. But baseball or no it was all Chuck-and-London.

Between seasons Chuck took London to meet his mother. She did not like to have a dog on her davenport. "But, Ma, at Kearney sometimes he eats at the table with the team!" It made no difference. She did not like to see a dog in the house. She loved having her son come, but after three days she was ready for them to go on their way.

They hunted grouse in Utah, they hunted deer in Wisconsin, pheasants in South Dakota. London hunted like a man and retrieved like a dog. Once when he was told to keep his nose for the birds, he chased a rabbit instead. For that he had to be disciplined like any dog.

A hunter and his dog make a team. The man with the license and the gun determines where they go, using his knowledge of the countryside and the habits of the game. The dog must confine himself to an area directly in front of the man and keep in contact. Here the dog's keen sense of smell locates the birds. Silently he points them out to the man who will flush them and shoot them.

Though a well-trained bird dog is not allowed to have anything to do with rabbits, London, on their tramps through the mountains, had often chased them, and Chuck only laughed, because he could never catch a dancing dodging little cottontail.

With a South Dakota license and a gun the two were hunting in earnest. A rabbit leaped from a tuft of bush. Off ran London after him.

"No!" shouted Chuck. "London!" he called. "London! come back here."

Up a hillside London followed the rabbit's zigzag course. Up and over, and he was out of sight. Ten minutes later he came back, without the rabbit of course, and with a cut foot. This part of South Dakota is barbed-wire country.

With both hands Chuck grasped the loose fold of skin along London's back. "When I tell you to come,"–he lifted the big dog bodily off the ground–"that's what I mean for you to do." But he did not give the dog his shaking. "Do you understand me?"

London would not struggle nor even whimper. He could not meet Chuck's eyes.

"When I'm talking to you, you look at me."

London looked.

Chuck put him down on his feet. The dog, tail hanging, stood looking at him out of the corner of his eyes. He made Chuck uncomfortable, standing motionless that way.

"And when I tell you 'No,' London, you'd better know I mean 'No!' Or I'll–oh, well . . ."

At that, London came to life and did his best to answer, making little dog noises in his throat and in his mouth. "I understand," he was agreeing.

"Do you understand?" asked Chuck.

They went on with their hunting.

In no time London jumped another rabbit. This one leaped up almost from under his feet. After all, London was still a dog and he did have instincts. He was off again.

Chuck did not try to call him back. He simply stood there and stared.

In perhaps a hundred yards London was suddenly brought up short by some unseen obstacle. Nothing was blocking his path. Yet his tail dropped, his ears went down. He turned and hurried back to where, hand on hip, Chuck stood waiting.

"Get over here."

Again a hand closed on the fold of skin. This time there was no attempt to lift the dog. Chuck's voice was quiet. "When I tell you . . ."

But he had said more than enough.

Never again was London to take off after either cottontail or jack rabbit, while he and Chuck were hunting together as a team.

Chuck and London drove to California. In Los Angeles Chuck directed athletics at a military school. Since he once had been a major in the United States Army, he was made commandant. When there was a parade he wore his medals. London stood at attention on the parade ground while cadets passed in review. He too had a medal of his own, with a ribbon to go with it, for perfect attendance.

But their best time was baseball season.

Despite their contract, Chuck and London, after the first year, did make road trips in the club bus. If Chuck was to pitch, it meant he could stretch out in the big bus that carried only fifteen or so passengers.

Once on a threatening afternoon the bus fell behind schedule. The boys were hungry and griping. Not only would there be no time to eat before the game, they would probably have to get into their uniforms on the bus.

Rain began to fall. The pavement glistened in the path of on-coming headlights. Some twenty miles short of their destination—McCook, Nebraska—the bus radio told of a storm ahead that laid down two inches of water.

"We'll have to verify this," decided Stickney. The bus pulled up at a roadside joint.

By telephone they learned the game was called on account of

rain. A game called is a hardship on the players. This one meant taking the rough two-hundred-mile trip all over on the first open date, which would otherwise have been their holiday.

A few beer guzzlers hurried out into the rain.

"Any of you guys want to eat here?"

"I don't wanna," said someone, voicing the feeling of all.

London was lying on the back seat.

"London," urged Chuck, "you've been on this bus three hours. You'd better go out. It's a long slow way home."

London yawned and dropped to his feet. He sauntered down the aisle, stopped and looked at the window. Cold drops chased each other down the darkened pane. Raindrops drummed on the roof. He turned back to Chuck.

"Go ahead."

"Aw–w–woo," yawned London and stretched. Then he too said it. "Aw–doaan–waana!"

He certainly made his feeling clear. It was only what his teammate had already said. As the dog curled up on the seat, the men were roaring with laughter.

The bus rolled along its homeward way. A merrier team struck up a song. Decks of cards broke out.

In the weeks to come Chuck carefully rehearsed London on his smash line. "Say, 'Ah doan wanna,' London, please." Chuck yawned to help him into the mood. "Ah–doaan–wanna!"

London, who knew the language well enough, did not speak it fluently. He tried. Out of these rehearsals he did hit upon another good line, his "How are you?" He was trying to say, "I don't want to." It came out, "Ow–aaah–uuu?" Chuck seized upon that one too. In time–a short time at that–Chuck helped him get both lines down pat. The dog knew when to use them too.

If a player handed him a dime and wanted a package of gum, and if Chuck did not object, London would buy him his gum and bring him his change. A player would ask, "London, get me a candy bar, please. Here's your money."

Of this candy bar London would not get a taste. Chuck forbade it. Though Chuck ate candy, he thought too much of London's teeth.

"Ah doaan waanna," yawned London.

London can glad-hand his way past any "No Pets" policy.

By now he was so completely one of the boys that he would have been put on the payroll, if only he too could have stood at the plate and swung a bat with any kind of an average at all.

London's fame spread.

Life magazine asked for a picture story on the dog who played baseball. A New York photographer was sent out West, into the wilds of Nebraska, to pose the dog. He got run-of-the-mill pictures: London wearing a baseball cap, London catching a batted ball, London jumping through Chuck's looped arms, London running to first base with a pitcher's jacket in his mouth. The shots were good enough for a story intended only for the oddities section in the back pages.

However, after the photographer got his pictures, and said good-by to the team, he stayed on, without saying anything about it to Chuck, who by this season was managing the Irishmen. He wanted to catch the afternoon game.

Even before this game began there was bad feeling on the part of the visiting team's manager. He was piqued because of a smart move Manager Eisenmann had just made. It was an important game in the pennant race between Kearney's Irishmen and Lexington's Minute Men; Chuck needed a left-handed pitcher to win. His friend, Fred Kipp, was serving a hitch in the Air Force in nearby Goodland, Kansas. For a hundred and fifty dollars Chuck was able to fly in the famed left-hander for this one game. Baseball is like this. A manager does anything he can to win. So does a player. Anything he can get away with.

The manager of Lexington's Minute Men did not like it at all.

Disaster struck in the fifth with the score a tie. The Irishmen were at bat; Pitcher Kipp singled. It had become London's customary role to take out the warmup jacket for any Irishman pitcher. No one was keener on baseball customs than London.

With Kipp's jacket in his mouth he ran out toward first base. This brought him his customary cheer and a big hand.

Lexington's manager decided not to like either London's presence on the diamond nor the cheer, which gave a boost to the Irishmen. He scowled at the umpire.

"Manley, you going to let a dog make a farce out of this game?"

Chief Umpire Manley also had a gripe. A week-old argument with Chuck smoldered. Manley had said a ball pitched by Chuck had hit a batter. Chuck had been quoted in the papers: "That ball never came within two feet of Haig Lavery. Manley is as blind as they come!"

The umpire wore a tolerant smile as he stepped up to block London's progress. "Give it to me." London, who respected the blue uniform of an ump, did as he was told.

Chuck came charging up from the third-base coaching box. Nobody, not even a chief umpire, was going to interfere with London when he was carrying out his appointed task. Not with Chuck around.

The stands loved that dog. "Smack him, Chuck!" And they liked a fight.

Chuck did not let them down. He jerked Kipp's jacket out of Manley's clutches and gave it back to his dog. Quickly London took it to Kipp, who waited on first. But when London walked back to where Umpire Manley and Lexington's disgruntled manager stood together, glaring, he was wary-eyed and ready for trouble.

Chuck called London to his side, turned his back on them, and walked away toward Kearney's dugout. At the coaching line he paused, breathing hard. "Go to your place, London." He was at the coaching box, ready for the next Irishman batter, when to his surprise, right on his heels, he saw the two umpires.

A good umpire does not follow a player into this territory. Manley, whatever his beef, had no business at the coaching line, since at the moment there was no play. Behind him stood the plate umpire.

Manley blurted to Chuck, "Get that dog off the field."

"You joking? I don't see any dog on the field. Maybe I'm blind too."

The eager fans spurred them on. "Boo-ooo! Boo-ooo! Boo-ooo!" They could not catch the words; they saw the waving arms; they wanted blows to be struck.

"Get him out of the park, then!" shouted Manley. "Get that dog right out of this park!"

Chuck could yell too. "What for? Why does my dog have to go?"

"Because I say so, that's what for!"

Chuck, whose temper had caused trouble in the past, knew how to control it when he was plainly in the right. And he knew too how a controlled loss of temper can make an even better show. London, on his feet and with blood in his eye, also was keeping himself under control behind the barricade. Nor had any other of Chuck's teammates rushed out to back him up, though he was being threatened by two angry umpires. The new manager had made it clear that when he was hassling with umpires their help was not welcome. With a roster of only fifteen he couldn't afford to have more than one man run out of the game.

Manley pulled a watch out of his pocket. He glowered at it. "I give you thirty seconds to get the dog off the field."

"I tell you," yelled Chuck, "there's no dog on the field. Can't you see anything?"

"Get that dog out of the park, then." Red in the face he raised his hand like a referee in a ring. "One!" he counted and down came his hand. "Two!" The hand was counting Chuck out.

If Chuck hit him he would get a suspension that would stick. And a fine. But the rule book says nothing against coming up close. And breathing hard. Chuck's big shoulders brushed the shorter man's head. Chuck's breath in the umpire's face was an offense. "You and your little watch!"

"Four! Five! The game–is–forfeited!"

The rule book states that a game is to be forfeited only as a last resort. All these people had paid their money. Chuck had been

offered thirty seconds. He had been given a count of five. Even a pugilist gets ten.

"Besides that," Manley went on, compounding his absurdity, "you're out of the game, Eisenmann."

Chuck laughed in his face. "The guy puts me out of a game already forfeited."

When the Irishmen heard that the game was forfeited, the way was clear for them to come swarming out of the dugout.

"Get going, Eisenmann. Gwan. I'll call the cops. Gwan get outta here!"

With these words Manley raised his fist. It was an umpire's classic gesture of dismissal, to wave a player to the showers. But Manley let that clenched fist pass too close to Chuck's nose.

Fearing a fist fight the plate umpire pushed his way between them. "Let me handle this, Manley."

If Chuck would take it, London definitely would not. Onto the field he too charged. With a snarl and a vicious show of teeth he lunged at the plate umpire, slamming his paws on his chest. Up in that position a German shepherd can kill. On his hind legs, as tall as the man, he bared fangs within inches of the man's throat.

All fight drained out of the threatened umpire. Chuck would not speak or move; to act now might touch London off. The men stood like statues. The umpire's hands hung limp at his sides. Even the stands were hushed.

There was a suspended moment in Kearney's stadium when of all the spectators only a single man moved. It was *Life*'s photographer, hurrying down the aisle, his press camera in both hands, working the gadgets as he ran. If a man is to be killed, a photographer thinks of pictures. If the man *is* killed, the pictures will be worth more. He was snapping as he ran, pictures through the wire.

London, his big paws planted squarely on the umpire's body, somehow got him turned around and began pushing him off the field. No one lifted a hand to stop him. He pushed the vanquished enemy all the way to the stands.

Spectators began pouring onto the field, in the photographer's wake. Among those milling about were three of the team's board of directors and Kearney's chief of police.

"Come with me, Chuck," urged the chief. "We'd better humor him." For even then the officials were hoping against hope that Manley could be persuaded to eat his words and save the day.

Chuck said, "Let's go, London."

It did not work. An umpire's ruling passion is to save face. And an umpire's decision is final.

Somebody made an announcement over the loud-speakers. The game was to go to Lexington by forfeit. The score, customary in forfeited games, was to be nine to nothing, in favor of Lexington. Anybody wanting his money back could call at the box office.

Somebody else got to the loud-speakers. The game would go on!

Regardless! But because of Manley's decision, it would not count. On the record Lexington would keep its technical victory, 9–0.

The game did go on. Kearney scored. The score did not count. A lot of the fans got their money back.

Umpire Manley insisted that Manager Eisenmann be suspended and fined two hundred and fifty dollars. The league president refused to suspend Eisenmann or to fine him, or to reprimand him in any way. Manley had no other course than to resign.

One clear note sounded above the unhappy echoes. In a few days *Life* magazine appeared. The story of London's rhubarb was given a place of prominence, in the news section up front. "London Embroiled," is *Life*'s caption. The unposed pictures, blurred with action, record even the expressions on men's faces.

London was a nation-wide celebrity.

CHAPTER EIGHT

Home Run

OUR PEOPLE want to see the dog. What will it take to bring London to Watertown?"

Chuck had expected this offer to be for himself, when the manager of the Watertown Sky Sox flew in from South Dakota. Instead it was for London, and for a one-night stand.

As soon as the price was right, Chuck began to have doubts. "How long a show?"

"You'll take the place of infield practice. Say half an hour. You can have as much time as you like, though."

"What'll we do with all that time?"

"You don't have to do anything. Stand out there with him. Our people want to see the dog."

Chuck and London had two weeks to prepare a routine for their allotted time. Chuck polished the car, packed in the props for London's performance, and they made the trip.

The show was scheduled for a Thursday night because Thursday was the poor drawing night of the week. Stores in town stayed open. The ball park needed an added attraction.

"Our best crowd in years!" said the ground keeper as he let Chuck's shining convertible into the park.

Tall in the back of the open car, London braced paws against the back of the front seat. Chuck drove him sedately around the outfield and parked in the glare of twenty-five lamps at the first-base coaching line. It surely did not look like an off night. There must have been close to three thousand people watching from the stands.

The president of the club conducted Chuck to the microphone. But all eyes stayed with the dog left in the open car.

With a game in progress Chuck was never at a loss for words. Now he was aware of the empty diamond behind him. He gripped the mike; he stuck closely to his prepared speech. Even so his mouth went dry.

"Enough of me," and finally he got himself off the hook.

He lifted his left arm and flipped his wrist. London jumped to the front seat, then out through the open door. Windmill tail flailing, he bounded to Chuck's side. He too was well-prepared, even to the point of boredom; he could climb the ladder that waited in the car, he could identify various household objects stashed away in a carton, he could take the key out of the car's ignition, bark out his age, do sums . . .

With London at his side Chuck was more at ease. "Ladies and gentlemen, meet my boy. Take a bow, London."

All at once London froze as though thunderstruck. He did not make his bow, nor did he keep his eyes on Chuck, but stared up into the stands. Perplexed, he turned at last to Chuck. "What's up?"

Fortunately Chuck's self-consciousness did not keep him from realizing what had happened. The loud-speakers in the stands had been slapping his mechanized voice back to the dog from up there. How could London obey a command that did not come from him, and was hardly in his voice?

"It's all right, Lon." He stepped out of range. "I'll be back with you in a moment. Hank!" he called into the microphone. Hank was Watertown's manager. "Take this mike for me. London doesn't get it. We're going to move back to home plate. When I talk to him you broadcast what I say."

So with the star and his straight man near home plate, and with Watertown's manager interpreting at the microphone, Chuck told London to take a bow.

London made his well-rehearsed bow.

"London, did you remember to lock the car? No? Do so, please. And bring me the key."

"London, did you remember . . ." Hank repeated the words over the public address system. Since these repeated words of Chuck's were in another's voice, London paid no attention to the loud-speakers. Anyway, he knew the routine by heart. Before Hank finished, he gave Chuck his most bored look, and was on his way. Clambering into the open car he bit gingerly at the metal ignition key, pulled it out and duly delivered it.

"Thank you."

The crowd clapped.

Chuck was rubbing London's head nervously when on a sudden impulse he said something not planned on. The car door was wide open. As though they were just talking, Chuck said, "London, is that the way you leave a parked car?"

Hank began repeating it. London wagged his tail at this unexpected break in the routine. He passed Chuck's hand lightly through his mouth to show appreciation and ran back to the car to shut the door.

That door was in need of a mechanic's attention. In the wide-out position it stuck; one had to lift up on it to make it close at all. London pushed with a paw. It stuck. He pushed with both paws. It was really stuck. Everyone in the audience was pushing with him when suddenly he backed up and rushed it. His ninety pounds slammed it with a bang.

The people were delighted. Amidst his cheers the cocky dog sauntered back to home plate.

"Next time," Chuck said, playing it straight, "don't break out the window."

London all but grinned at him.

Right there in the beginning of the Watertown act, Chuck scrapped his carefully prepared program. He would still have it to fall back on, if the light went out of their ad-libbing. He sincerely wanted to make these people see how he and his dog talked together. Oh, he could say to London, "Bring me a ball," and London would fish a ball out of their carton, or "Bring me my glove," or, "London, what is it I use when I wipe the dishes?" And they would be made aware of his knowledge of words. But it was more than that! He wanted to make them see how he and London could communicate. And London was showing with every line of his body that he was willing and ready.

"London," asked Chuck, "do you know where you are?"

Here was a concept he had never before put into words with his dog, but it was within London's power.

Even Chuck could never quite get used to the way his dog would respond. London looked about him, not at the stands now, but at the two dugouts, then at the diamond behind him. To London, the best of all places in the outdoor world was a baseball diamond. His tail wagged a little.

The people could not help but see something of this. Probably to many of them it would be merely another sign that the man had rehearsed his dog well. It would do no good for Chuck to have Hank broadcast: "My dog has never before been asked this question."

Chuck went on, "Suppose, London, suppose out there on this diamond a game is going on. Suppose you are on the team. London, you're playing baseball!"

The spell was on them both. Chuck told himself, go slow! go slow! they must be made to see it. If it happens too fast, it will look like just another trick. If the stands could be made to see . . .

"London, the Irishmen are at bat!"

"London, the Irishmen are at bat!" The words came back to them from the public address system. This did not break the spell.

It helped fashion it. London's ears were stiff; Chuck held his undivided attention.

"Suppose, London, you are at bat! Now, mind you, London, this is a hypothetical situation." Chuck's heart was beating fast, but he saw he had his dog with him. Hypothetical indeed! He knew London's admiration for big words. The dog was saying, silently, "Well! This *is* something new!"

"Step up to the plate, London. That's right. Face the mound." It was more than make-believe. London did step up to the plate. London did face the mound.

"Here comes the pitch, London! The ball is in your power!" Chuck's mind was wholly on the dog, no longer even hearing Hank rebroadcast the talk. As for the dog, he had long shown his ability to carry out the man's will.

"You swing, London. You clout it. London! London! You've just hit a home run. You've hit the ball out of the park."

Key words here. Home run. Ball out of the park. London knew those phrases, but he knew more, far more, of what Chuck had in mind.

"Then what are you waiting for, London? You've hit your homer. Go ahead."

At that command London had to take over. He would do something; he would act now; but what he would do Chuck could not be quite sure. It was all a gamble...

The dog always delayed a moment before carrying out a complicated order. It was as though he had to go back over all Chuck had said to him. London looked down at his feet; like a batter's, they were at home plate. Chuck looked down too. Just as Chuck was feeling he had tried for too much, and was casting about for something different, London turned toward the beaten path that leads to first.

Suddenly he was galloping to first base, and in the stands people got to their feet. At first base London hit the bag and swung, full speed, toward second, and everybody up there was seeing it too.

Not a performing dog! More! A batter was racing on his triumphant way. Again he touched the bag, at second, and headed for third.

At third London made his error. He swung wide of the base bag. He knew better than that. Endless talk with Chuck, countless hours of watching the game, had told him what bases are for. But at third base, probably a different picture was in his mind. Here, near third, was where Chuck would be coaching, if the Irishmen were at bat, Chuck waiting to give a home runner a quick shake of the hand as he passed the third-base coaching box. At any rate, London ran wide of the bag there by the coaching box.

Now he entered the home stretch. Now the runner slacked off. There was no question about it—he was aping players who knock home runs and turn lackadaisical after rounding third, slowing down to bask in the applause.

Here in the dugout London saw a real team. They were not Irishmen, but they were not make-believe. Here were players waiting for a real game to begin. London looked at them as he loped by their dugout. "Boys," one could imagine him calling out, "how did you like the way I rapped that one? Boys, this is the easy route."

The last few yards brought him home in a gallop.

He sat down beside Chuck. His big bushy tail brushed dust off home plate. Out of the corner of his eye he caught Chuck's approval.

The roar from above was deafening.

When at last Chuck could make himself heard, he said, "London!"

"London!" said all the loud-speakers.

The spotlights were on London. Contrasting with his glowing dark coat, dark with a hint of rust, those two broad white bands back of his shoulder blades, reaching down to his white chest, gave him a theatrical appearance.

"London, if I were Chief Umpire Manley . . ."

This time the laugh was for Chuck.

". . . I would call you out at third."

London raised that light eyebrow of his.

"No, London, don't question an umpire. You still have time, though. It's not too late for you to go back to third base and correct your error. You can still earn your run."

London studied Chuck. He looked away to third.

"Go do it, then."

The dog got to his feet. Trotting toward third, he paused. In a hushed stadium he looked back to Chuck. "Is this what you mean?" Lightly he ran on, the rest of the way. Instead of touching third base with a paw and coming home, the clown sat down on the bag and let his tongue hang out.

A wave of Chuck's hand brought him in.

The people of Watertown were ready to believe anything.

"Any questions?"

"Any questions?" blared the loud-speakers.

One man in the stands did not need a microphone, "Mister," he shouted down. "How old is that dog?"

"London, a man wants to know your age. How old are you?"

To the dog it was a real letdown. "Bark, bark," he began. "Bark, bark, bark." A moment later he merely woofed.

"Says he's five and a half."

The man was still on his feet. He seemed to think the laugh was for him. "Mister, how does a dog learn all that?"

Here was the question Chuck needed to answer. "You have to talk with your dog," he began earnestly. "You ought to talk with your dog every chance you get . . ."

"Well," interrupted the man, "I been talking with my dog all his life, and he still don't know a thing."

Chuck took over the microphone.

"All right!" he said, into the laughter. "All right." He wanted these people to know why London understood.

"I mean," he said, when he could be heard, "I mean talk with him on a human level."

But that only set them off again, all the louder.

Nothing he could say could add to what London had already told them. And anyway, their half hour was nearly gone. The rest of it sort of petered out. A boy wanted London to do a sum; London barked out the right answer. There was magic to this, but it looked more like a trick.

It was time for the baseball game to take over.

Within days every club in the area was clamoring for the dog.

One of the shows that followed was seen by a woman who wrote in to the "You Asked for It" television program. She asked for the dog who thinks like a man.

Her letter opened up, for London and for Chuck, Hollywood's golden gate.

CHAPTER NINE

Camera!

FOR ART BAKER'S television show, "You Asked for It," London and Chuck were given a small assignment. They were to act out a skit, first of several which comprised his half-hour show.

Chuck suggested that London act as his secretary. He explained how his dog was at his best without rehearsal. Art Baker was not convinced. "Just have him run through a couple of his duties."

So, shortly before they were to go on the air, Chuck said, "London, will you lower the blind, please?" London knew Venetian blinds. He went over and pulled the cord. The whole thing collapsed on his head. "London, please bring me the wastebasket." London's teeth got caught in the wire mesh. "London, will you please bring me my coat." The top-heavy coat rack fell on him.

Chuck lost his temper.

Art Baker placed a practiced arm around his broad shoulders. "We'll make the prop men steady the props."

The prop men were pounding in a last nail when the red lights warned. Chuck was soothed; London was in place on a straight-backed chair before a typewriter. Cameras were swung into focus; powerful lights glared; a monstrous sound-boom was lowered over the dog's head. Yet he sat there, with perfect presence, apparently mindful only of what he was about to compose on the white paper before him.

The show went on the air.

"Take a letter, London, please."

Chuck dictated a message to the city fathers, protesting the Los Angeles leash law. Big dogs should have mental leashes. When a strong dog and a weak owner are chained together, it is the human who is on a leash. London slapped away at the keys, balancing himself by pushing one paw against the machine, typing with his left as he leaned studiously over his work. The camera registered the little black marks which began to appear on the white paper. The lights brought out the contrast of snow-white paws against the black machine, the contrasts in London's coat. Under his fine dark forehead his eyes shone. His white cheeks, his dark nose, his large stiff ears and those two distinguishing broad white bands over his shoulders gave TV screens all across America a memorable image.

London's whole attention was on his typing. Never once did he glance at the technicians.

"Don't hunt and peck, London. Get that letter out. Use both hands."

No longer permitted to steady himself with his right paw, London slapped heavily at the keyboard with both paws. Typewriter

keys bunched in a tangle. The sound-boom swung low to pick up the jangling noise. Art Baker injected stage laughter.

"Faster," ordered Chuck.

London pounded away furiously.

"Ha, ha, ha," laughed Art Baker. "Chuck, may I borrow your secretary? Mine's not half this good. Ha, ha, ha."

Chuck said, "London, bring me the letter, please."

A million and more viewers saw the dog get up on the chair, draw the paper out of the machine with his teeth and carry it across the room to where Chuck sat at an executive desk. It did not matter that, once in a newspaper office, London had done this trick before; somehow the lights and the camera and the anxious studio officials lent the needed excitement; he put on an inspired show.

Chuck said, "No mistakes, I see, London. Now may I have an envelope?"

When the dog went over to the steel filing cabinet to pull out a drawer and hunt for an envelope, Art Baker interrupted. "Terrific!" London could tune out other people, but this man was an authority here. "Simply terrific, London!" As though spoken to by an umpire at a game, London quit looking for the envelope. Chuck had to remind him, "London! I still don't have my envelope!"

The second steel drawer London pulled out slid all the way open. It fell on his paws. Making nothing of the hurt, he found the envelope in it and took it to Chuck.

London helps Art Linkletter with his "House Party" show.

Without being told, he picked up a crumpled sheet of paper and put it in the wastebasket. He shook the small rug. At Mr. Baker's relayed request he dialed the telephone, holding the receiver in his mouth. When Baker gave Chuck the cue that time was up and Chuck told London, "We'll quit for the day," London brought his coat, from a rack now nailed down, turned off the lights and closed the door behind them. The show was left to Art Baker's chuckles of wonder.

The world of television, always hungry for material, pounced upon the dog. The Art Baker program was rebroadcast; other programs were offered Chuck. A producer who saw in London a born trooper formed a new company to film a series of television episodes built around London. After shooting thousands of feet of film, the company decided the material was too big for television; they would create a full-length motion picture.

London found a place for Chuck in motion pictures. Chuck wears the stocking cap in this scene from *The Littlest Hobo*.

To change objectives in midstream is expensive; little of the old footage could be used. However, London's talents promised to help greatly in the economy. On location he proved to be many dogs in one. Other movie dogs not only require stand-ins; they have doubles to share the acting. One Lassie is an attack dog; another jumps and does Lassie stunts; still another Lassie is featured in close-ups. London not only had as fine a face as any in Hollywood; he could play every part.

The new script was sketchy, depending on London to help develop the story. The company did not hire a story writer. It seemed enough to say, "Let's have London save a little boy's pet lamb from the slaughterhouse!" Hollywood knows how to pad out an idea like this with endless police chases.

Since sheep are cheap, three cinema stars were selected from a flock in the Mojave Desert to play the title role. That first working title did not belong to London. It was, "The Miracle of the Lamb."

At nine o'clock one sunny Saturday morning a new director, a cameraman, and three or four members of the producing company waited on location with Chuck and London for the lambs to be trucked in. Time was short and the budget low. The shooting location was a shipyard which could be rented only for the week end while shipbuilders were off duty.

At last the trailer brought in three frightened lambs. The only preparation these newcomers had for stardom was a short length of rope tied around the neck of each. No one of the lambs had seen much of humans until this day, save for their lone Basque shepherd.

"Which lamb do we start with?"

"Let London choose."

When the lambs saw a strange wolflike dog sniffing at their trailer they bleated in terror and banged their woolly bodies against the far side. London considered them through the slats. They were much alike, white lambs with dark markings around their faces, chosen for their similarity so that when one tired, another could take its place. Some ancestral memory was stirring the shepherd dog's blood. He ran around the trailer, hopping high on hind legs, trying for a better view, glancing back at Chuck in disbelief.

This was going to be the kind of work he was cut out for!

A man called Frosty, not a studio hand but an all-round expert and trouble shooter who had money in the company, let down the tail gate. Right away a lamb jumped out, scampering off to hide amidst the debris.

Chuck closed the end gate. By now he had worked long enough with film people to think twice before volunteering help. A signal kept his dog at his side while Frosty and a couple of the men took after the escapee.

For the two cowering creatures in the trailer, London had only contempt. He knew which lamb he wanted; he wanted the lamb that got away.

"Wait," Chuck steadied him.

The men chased crazily. The lamb popped in and out over machinery, over coils of rope, around piled-up junk, while three men came stumbling after. The scared animal leaped onto a pile of scrap lumber, only to hop down again before anybody could get close.

At last Chuck had to yell to them. "Hey! Cut it out! You'll kill him. Let the dog bring him in."

The men were glad enough to give up.

"A sheep gets winded," explained Chuck. "He's fat. He could just lie down and die."

"What about us?" panted Frosty.

"All right, London. Bring me your lamb."

Off he ran, with the short barks of the chase. When he had circled the area, he moved cautiously, cutting off escape, sewing the lamb in. When he had his quarry cornered in a narrow corridor of crates, he stopped to send back a look. What to do next?

Three men started toward him to make the capture.

Chuck stopped them. "No. Let the dog finish his task." He called to London, "Bring him in."

London disappeared among the big storage boxes. Soon his wagging tail came into sight. He was backing out, dragging his prize. When he backed into full view, there, taut in his jaws, was the short end of stout rope, and there, a moment later, the head of the lamb, and finally the whole resisting animal, fighting for every inch, digging sharp little hoofs at the concrete.

The script called for a lamb thankful to the dog for saving its life. The mood of this tug-of-war was all wrong.

One of the two lambs shut up in the trailer bleated. Instantly the rebellious one changed its attitude. He became a poor little lamb wanting only to be a sheep among sheep, and lunged toward the trailer. Now came London's turn to hold back. With the end of the rope clamped securely in his jaws he forced his charge to walk, not run. Before they had progressed half way, the lamb resigned his fate to this headstrong guide. Obediently he minced along at London's side as though this were an everyday occurrence.

It made good theater, a resolute dog convoying a lost lamb nearly

as large as himself. The lamb too was a handsome fellow in black and white. Brilliantly white was his fleece in the sunshine. His ears, his snout, and his big round eyes were black as ink, and black were his four prancing feet.

"Chuck!" cried the excited director, "it's just what we need. Have you got the script in mind?"

"Sure. London and I have been over your outline."

The director looked at the sky. Off to the west a lumpish cloud was forming. Mostly the sun shone hot in smogless blue.

"That cloud out there," he demanded of the cameraman. "Is it going to cover the sun?"

The man with the big tripod held up a square of colored glass and squinted at the skies. "You've got twenty minutes anyhow," was his decision.

"Chuck. Scene 42. Where the dog hides the lamb in the stateroom. When your dog is ready we'll shoot it."

So is a film made. Begin in the middle, begin at the end, begin even at the beginning if the signs are right. Of course everybody would prefer to begin at the beginning; it is easier to keep the story in mind. But in practice you might have to begin with Scene 42, and that's what a director is for.

"The dog will be ready once we walk over the course."

"All right, go ahead. Listen, everybody. Here's the setup. Frosty hides back of that shed with the lamb. While Chuck walks his dog over the course, Abernathy, you drive that trailer out of camera shot, and, when I give the signal, make one of those lambs bleat. We're not shooting for sound. It'll help London with his lamb."

Abernathy shrugged. "Anybody round here tell me how you make a lamb bleat?"

"Who needs a bleat?" laughed Chuck. "London won't need help." While he walked with his dog, he warned London to be careful of nails in the jumble of old lumber and told him how always he must keep in mind the menace of the police. "Remember, Lon, they've got orders to shoot to kill!"

A director embarrassed London by suddenly opening a door while the dog was practising how to make a lamb lie down.

An abandoned excursion steamer creaked against the pilings of a wharf, a once-gay vessel rotting in this backwater, waiting for the torches of a salvage crew. Tipped off-center, the doomed ship pushed tiredly at dock timbers, opening and closing a dark and yawning gap to the ebbing tide. The door of one of the decaying outer staterooms hung open. In there London was to hide his lamb. The police, said the plot, were hot on his trail, not only for stealing a lamb from the slaughterhouse, but because he had been reported as a mad dog at large.

When he and Chuck reached the place where the vessel's deck creaked closest to the timbers, Chuck said, "Look around, London, before you come aboard. Think you'll be able to pull the lamb with you up here? Don't you fall in! Put your paws up on the edge of the ship."

Since they would not be shooting for sound, Chuck could hide himself near here, out of range of the camera, and tell London the rest of what he had to do while the scene was being shot. If anything went wrong, the camera could always be stopped, the scene cut, to be picked up again where they left off. But Chuck did not want any cuts. The weaker the actor, the more cuts for further direction. Chuck wanted it all to be taken in a single sequence, so that people could see how his dog could keep on acting until the end of the scene was filmed.

He called to the director, "Okay, Ron. We're ready." Then he sent London racing back to the shed where Frosty was holding his lamb out of sight.

"Ready, Frosty?"

"Ready!"

"Action!"

"Let's go, London."

From behind the shed, where he had gone to join Frosty and the lamb, the dog appeared, alone at first, to take a few cautious steps into the sunshine.

"You'll have to come forward more," shouted Chuck. "Look around. Don't look at me." This brought the dog over a pile of rope, past a rusting anchor. "Stop. Look for those cops. Now come, faster. Run, London! Run up here close to the ship."

Close to the ship there was no Chuck to be seen. He was behind the funnel.

London reached the place where the creaking deck eased nearest to the wharf. "That's it. Put your paws on the edge of the deck." The ship pulled away a little, widening the gap, alarming the dog. "London, I said paws up!" First one paw, then the other, rested against the rotting deck as the ship slowly rose and fell. London's ears were at their stiffest as he looked up and down the deck. The camera would register a dog searching for a hiding place for his lamb. When his sight fastened on the half-open cabin door forward, Chuck ordered, "Hold it!" London froze. On films this would say he had found the hiding place.

"Now go back, London. Get your lamb. Quick! The cops!"

Leaping over obstacles London raced for the shed. Chuck again called, "Hold it!" He did not want the dog to disappear from sight entirely. That would be like cutting the scene in the middle for further direction. Only London's head and shoulders were behind the shed when Chuck asked, "Frosty! Does he have the rope?"

"Okay, Chuck."

"Okay, London. Bring your lamb."

London tugged. Chuck called, "Frosty! Give that lamb a good push from behind!"

Out with a start came the lamb, suddenly willing to follow London's lead. With a short hitch London pulled the bewildered creature, guiding him over their obstacle course. They reached the spot where London had rested paws on the deck's edge.

"Jump aboard!"

London leaped. There was power enough in his neck and shoulders to make the lamb jump with him. They were safely aboard.

"Turn right, London. Put the lamb in the cabin!" As the two hurried on past the funnel hiding Chuck from view, he reminded the dog, "When you get him in there, lock the door on him. Now hurry! The cops!"

The dog was called on to race forward with his charge, crowd the animal into the little stateroom, turn him loose in the dark of the cabin, and leave him in there while he went out and slammed the door behind him.

Chuck called, "Come back, London. No, not to me. Up those steps." Rusting iron steps led to an upper deck. "Climb the steps. Get out of the picture."

The steps in the sun were burning hot. London's exit was made in haste.

"Okay," said the director.

Chuck came out of hiding. He raced up the iron steps, to find London panting in the shade of the superstructure. He lay down beside his dog and stroked the back of his head, rubbed him under the chin.

"Terrific!" came a voice from below. "Terrific," someone else echoed. London whimpered a little, and his brown eyes which

London fraternizes with the other professional in his *The Littlest Hobo*—the Judas goat who leads the lambs to slaughter.

through the years had grown warmer with understanding asked, "Was I really good?"

"You were the greatest."

Down the steps came Chuck with the dog star in his arms. The men crowded around, each to add his word of praise.

"He's my boy." Chuck put the embarrassed dog on the ground. "Just a born ham."

The director, new with the company, said, "Chuck, I'm the first to admit your dog is terrific. We're all great. But time is short. Now let's shoot it."

"Shoot it?" Chuck was puzzled.

"Shoot the scene. Get it down on film. We're making a picture, you know."

"You mean you didn't get that down on film? You mean to tell us . . ." Chuck's lips tightened, his hands drew into fists. Had London's performance been lost completely? Wasted! Thrown away! Merely because an ignorant fool wanted to save film! ". . . you had those animals in front of your camera for that whole scene and you didn't even let the camera grind?"

In picture making there is no valid argument against a man with a higher salary. "Bud," said the director to Chuck, but he did not meet his eye, "you've got a lot to learn about making pictures!"

"Mister," said Chuck, controlling his temper, "you've got a lot to learn about animals."

The director could have countered, "How much do *you* earn?" He was something of a gentleman so he put it this way, "How many pictures have *you* made?"

Frosty came between them. "Chuck is right, Ron. In this dog we have something special. From now on the camera's got to grind whenever London is on. Even rehearsals. Get it all down. The cheapest thing on our budget is the film."

A cloud had come over the sun. They all adjourned for lunch. After the break, London performed again, doing all he had acted

When London made this jump from a stockyard fence in *The Littlest Hobo*, he sprained his ankle on a loose board. He went right on with the action, but he limped.

out before. The second time he was almost, but not quite, as good as when the full excitement had been upon him.

His second performance of that particular sequence is what audiences still thrill to today. No third take was necessary. For most of the scenes wherein London appears, and he is on stage during three-fourths of the footage, the first take was the one to survive.

London's first picture was not released as *The Miracle of the Lamb*. Fleecy the Lamb was not the star; nor was there any single lamb called Fleecy. Before the picture was in the cans London had used up eight different lambs. The picture belonged to London, and so did the title. As *The Littlest Hobo*, it is still showing in neighborhood theaters.

The Littlest Hobo is a Grade-B picture. Made with a low budget, it is listed high by exhibitors; in the trade it is known as a sleeper. That is, a picture which makes more money than was expected.

London is asked to say a few words on his arrival in Dallas for the world premier of his second motion picture, *My Dog Buddy*.

CHAPTER TEN

Dog Star

EACH MAN who gives his heart to a dog must realize how the time will come, and is never far distant, when there will be a leave-taking. Seven times as fast as a man, a dog races to the end of the journey. London at twelve is as old as Chuck will be in his eighties; a very youthful eighty, however, for London is alert and wise, though he is getting gray.

Once, on a hunting trip in the Dakotas, Chuck, accepting this fate he was powerless to halt, left London for a short visit with a well-bred German shepherd who was chosen to mother London's pups. He was planning as he could for London's immortality. When the pups were nine months old he took possession of the male dog which most resembled the father.

Nine months, according to Chuck, is the ideal age to take on a new dog. Serious training should not commence before that age, save for a few must-nots. Even a puppy must not put paws on a lady's white dress. As a whole, the early months are better left to the breeder, who is less likely to force a young dog's mind or his frame.

Thorne, son of London, was nine months old when he came to live with his father and with Chuck. Already he was enough like his famed sire to serve as his stand-in. Thorne's skull is not so massive nor are the distinguishing white stripes across his shoulders so theatrical, but he has the same white contrasts at the sides of the face, the white powerful chest, and, until the camera closes in, the two dogs are indistinguishable on black-and-white film.

Before the younger dog came to share their bachelor quarters Chuck explained the situation to London. There would have been no fighting, regardless. An adult male dog is too chivalrous to take advantage of an adolescent. From the start London behaved to his son like a tolerant father.

In the dark before morning he woke Chuck by tapping on the side of the bed, a signal from far-off times, used for one purpose only.

"But London," objected the sleepy man, "this is not like you." He got up and opened the door for his dog, only to see London walk back to his bed and lie down. It was young Thorne who hurried past and ran out to the tall grass beyond the parking lot. Thorne who had been too timid to wake their man.

With London's and Chuck's help, Thorne learned fast. There was work for him too. Now that London is old and famous he needs his stand-in. He needs his stunt dog to run and jump for him.

A script called for London to leap off a bridge onto a truck passing below, then off the fast-moving truck into the line of traffic to be a casualty on the pavement when the camera moved in. Thorne did the hard part; London played dead for the close-up.

Thorne made his difficult jumps without hesitation, but, as is the custom in picture making, the director wanted it all done over again. A second time Thorne leaped atop the moving truck. A second time he jumped off the truck. But Thorne wanted to do everything his father could do, not just the hard parts. When the camera moved in, there on the pavement lay not one but two dead dogs.

A year after Thorne, Toro, son of London by Kola of Santa Monica canyon, joined the household. Toro has a long face and big black ears, yet he does resemble London.

A year later a fourth bed had to be made in the house. Chuck had not intended to take on a fourth dog; his hand was forced when one of London's latest offspring grew up to be his double.

And bright too! As this is written, Littlelon has been one of the boys but a matter of weeks, yet already this yearling imitates the other dogs in wanting to do whatever Chuck has in mind. When he sees Toro shut the door, he wants to shut the door. If Chuck opens the door for him to have a try, he is as likely to push from the wrong side, opening the door wider.

Three sons of London are eager to understand all that is said to them. They are proving Chuck's theory that talk is better than commands. Chuck directs them, not in obedience-school methods, but by speaking to them as to people, and he gets a personal response from each. Their capacity for the language seems to be in direct proportion to the time spent in this unique household.

Yet no matter how long he stays with Chuck, no one of London's sons will ever become the dog his father is. The difference between London and every other dog is London's central idea. Once upon a time, when Chuck saw his world come to nothing, he turned to a young dog for understanding. By accident he almost killed the dog. He vowed then and there he would never leave London. London and Chuck belonged to each other entirely at a crucial time in their lives, and they achieved a common language to a degree probably never before attained between man and beast.

Some day the story of London will be made the basis for a great picture. There is magic in London's struggle to bend his wild instincts and all his native cunning to the will of a man, at last making the man's work, baseball, his work. One has only to see Chuck and London together to feel it.

London is a dog-sitter in his third picture, *Just Between Us.*

The three productions in which London has starred have not even hinted at the real story. The movies Hollywood has built around him are plotted instead on motives truer to the world of color cartoons than to real life. London gives inspired performances, but he is made to act out plot incidents alien to his dog nature. As a hero, his unbelievable function is merely to go through life doing various Boy-Scout-type good turns, doing good to utter strangers. Even so his performance is a joy to watch.

There come moments in his pictures when he seems able to make plot as well as foreground completely his own. A memorable instance is the opening of *The Littlest Hobo.* The littlest hobo jumps out of a boxcar at the end of the journey. In the railroad yards he shakes the dust of the road from his coat. He locates a water faucet and gets himself a drink. A man is hosing down windows of empty Pullman cars. London accosts him and has his shower from the hose. The camera takes time to watch him shake himself dry. He wanders to a nearby eating joint where the proprietor is rolling down the awning. The man looks in surprise to see the big dog pick up trash from the sidewalk and place it neatly into the can. Who can resist giving London his handout?

Just as we feel we are in the presence of greatness, the screen calls on us to believe that London, on seeing a little boy weeping because he has to sell his pet lamb to the slaughterhouse, thereupon resolves that, come what will, he, London, will save the lamb and comfort the boy.

If ever the story of London's life is filmed, it will not be acted out by London himself. Already the dog is too old. Nor will Thorne be cast as the lead; Thorne is too eager. Toro is too big. The baby of the family, Littlelon, at present seems destined for the role.

Littlelon, who, more than either of the other sons has a will of his own, has all the advantages. He has Chuck, and London, and Thorne, and Toro, to point the way.

"Well boys, how's for a run on the sand?"

On his personal appearance tour for his third picture, *Just Between Us*, London has to travel by air.

There is a stretch of beach at the mouth of Santa Monica canyon called the Will Rogers State Beach. Here the sand is wide and clean and dogs are permitted. At the edge of the coast highway Chuck opened the car door. Littlelon first, then his half-brothers, then

Father London, jumped out to sniff around in the growth of green ice-plant covering the slope between pavement and sand.

London left them to return to Chuck, who sat watching from the open car. He reached in to take hold of Chuck's wrist. "Let's go."

The five walked down together among the sunbathers. At the tide line the sand was brown and hard. A wave pushed up to their feet, then fell away.

London looked at Chuck. "Now may I swim?"

The sun was hot; there would be time for the dogs to dry themselves. Chuck nodded.

Yipping in glee, the four dogs hit the water together. Only London headed out to sea; he jumped a frothy breaker, hurrying outward through the foam to be ready for the next, which was big enough to roll him. At the right moment he heaved himself high. The curling wave slapped his belly, and he was out beyond it, swimming now in the clear. He does not like to dive under waves any more. He doesn't like water in his ears.

Thorne, Toro, and Littlelon, were content to romp together in the shallows.

After their swim they were not permitted to roll in the sand. Chuck is as careful of their coats as any guardian is of his actors' wardrobes.

Five abreast they walked along the water's edge to a jetty of rocks. On the beach only now and then will someone recognize London and come up to Chuck for an autograph. All at once a boxer came bounding up, dragging his leash. Even if the boxer wanted only to play, the dogs were not allowed to associate with unknown canines. Chuck could not risk having their faces scarred, or their ears torn. Once Thorne had killed a challenger, slashing his throat.

Ever since, on their walks, Chuck has carried a short length of stout bamboo. "Sit!" Four dogs sat on the sand. Before the boxer came within striking distance, Chuck warned, "Stay away, you."

Thorne bristled. London only grinned, for he was already discovering that this was a female. A wave of Chuck's bamboo turned her. Up on the dry sand a woman was calling for her dog to come back and be tied. But the boxer only raced farther away along the hard wet sand, chasing the shadows of gulls.

"Dumb dog," each of the five friends said to himself, each in his own language.

On the beach they meet many people; there is nothing like a dog to break the ice, and four dogs are four times as good at it. Some of these people become friends. Nearly always a new friend will ask, "How come you never got married, Chuck?"

Chuck will snort, "What time have I got for a wife?"

On his personal appearance tour London is guest of honor at breakfast with the Governor of Louisiana.

He is still a young man, with unwritten chapters to his life. At present, his focus is on the care and feeding of his boys, their television work, their picture-making and their personal apppearances on the stage.

He is still a ball player too. Now and then on a Sunday he pitches a game for the All Stars. At Los Angeles' Wrigley Field the young

Rehearsing a script.

dogs have to wait in the car while he and London march together into the stadium. The off-season crowd is small, though this afternoon men on this diamond bear big names in baseballdom.

"Hello, Chuck! It's been a long time!"

"Hi, Chuck, where's London?"

"He's in the dugout. He'll be glad to see you again."

In the locker room after the game a table is spread with sandwiches, cheese, olives, hot dogs, cold milk, and hot coffee. And, for those who want it, iced bottles of beer.

"London," asks the caterer, "another hot dog?"

Sometimes Chuck has to warn him, "London, don't overdo just because it's free."

Back at the car they find the others, wagging their whole bodies, waiting to jump out and greet their two men of the world.

Printed in the USA
CPSIA information can be obtained
at www.ICGtesting.com
LVHW080423071123
763186LV00005B/374